Cent-sible
Homemaking

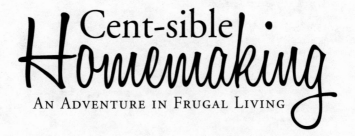

Cent-sible Homemaking

An Adventure in Frugal Living

Jean Clark

Tate Publishing & Enterprises

Published by Tate Publishing & Enterprises, LLC

127 E. Trade Center Terrace | Mustang, Oklahoma 73064 USA

1.888.361.9473 | www.tatepublishing.com

Tate Publishing is committed to excellence in the publishing industry. The company reflects the philosophy established by the founders, based on Psalm 68:11,
"The Lord gave the word and great was the company of those who published it."

Book design copyright © 2008 by Tate Publishing, LLC. All rights reserved.
Cover design by Kellie Southerland
Interior design by Jonathan Lindsey

Published in the United States of America

ISBN:978-1-60604-064-5

1. House & Home: Cleaning & Caretaking   2. Cooking: General/ Methods
08.03.18

Dedication

I dedicate this book in memory of my mother, Helen Pottle; my mother-in-law, Carolyn Clark; and my husband's grandmother, Doris Sleeper who were all great cooks. My mother knew I was writing this book, but passed away before it was published. Each of these special women taught me the value of cooking, thrift, and homemaking.

Acknowledgments

My sincere thanks go to my loving and supportive husband, Steve, and my daughter, Sarah, for encouraging me and helping me to make this book possible. Also, to my sons who knew of my interest in writing and have also encouraged me. I hope this book will be passed down to my grandchildren, their children, and their grandchildren, so that they might know a little about the importance of the Lord in their life, as well as the value of family and home. I also thank the Lord for all three of my children: Chris, Andy, and Sarah, and their wonderful spouses: Stacy, Joanna, and Andrew. I couldn't have chosen better spouses for my children than they did. I am thankful that the Lord has also blessed us with five beautiful grandchildren: Abbie, Emily, Connor, Simon, and Lillian.

Contents

Introduction

I don't know when my love for homemaking began; maybe it was the day I got married thirty-six years ago. I can't ever remember aspiring to be a housewife, mother, or homemaker. That would have been much too boring for my adventurous nature, but that's what the Lord had for me—I'm now the mother of three grown children. Many years ago, I imagined that I would one day write a book on homemaking and include my favorite recipes to pass along to my kids. My hope was that they would find it useful in creating and maintaining their own households. It was at least sixteen years ago that I started jotting down many of my hints for thrifty homemaking and putting together my favorite recipes. Nearly eleven years ago, my husband had the opportunity to work in Central America for a while. So I left my part-time job and we moved to Honduras where we resided for fourteen months. While in Honduras I was free to at least start my long thought-about book. It was in Honduras that I realized how helpful it was that I had good skills in "from scratch" cooking and improvising, and also had the opportunity to put hospitality into action. I'm so thankful to the Lord for those opportunities as well as meeting and observing a very poor local family in Honduras. Even though they had only cardboard on a dirt floor for beds, the mom was an example of good mothering and homemaking skills. She managed to spend time with her children, even though preparing of basic foods was difficult and time consuming. She had to dry and grind her own coffee beans, and cook her red beans, since they couldn't afford canned beans. In order to have chicken to eat, they had to kill and dress the chicken, if they could afford to have one. Also an example of how different her life as a homemaker was is that she had to make a broom out of a branch, attaching smaller branches with leaves to it just to sweep her dirt floor. Bath time was standing under a faucet outside of a building or using a small basin filled with water. There was not a lot of privacy! This wonderful Christian mom, in her poor village home, maintained neatness, cleanliness, and met the basic needs of her family of five children.

One of my main interests has always been feeding my family well on a budget and running the household economically. Also, it has always been important to me to decorate our home on a budget so that it would be comfortable for family and friends. Most importantly as a wife and mom, we need to meet our family's needs by providing good healthy food, a comfortable bed for good rest, discipline, manners, and lots of love. Hospitality is an interest that has developed over the years into a ministry for me. I worked part-time most of my adult life so I know that my hints can work for more than just women who are "at home" homemakers. My hope is to pass on enough good money-saving ideas for meal planning and home decorating so that other moms will be able to either stay at home with their children or work outside the home as little as they desire.

The time with your children is short, the years go by so fast, and soon they become adults. It's so important to take the time to teach them good values, ethics, and economical skills for their life's journey. I didn't always do things right while raising my children, but in retrospect I have learned to ask forgiveness for the things I didn't do so well and the wisdom to pass on what would have been the better choices.

The information contained in this book is not that of an advanced scholar. Rather, it is what I have learned by doing, usually through trial and error. Information I have gleaned from friends, relatives, and reading is also my source. I was blessed to have had a wise and efficient mother, and to have known and been taught by my late mother-in-law and also my husband's late "Grammy Sleeper." When I was first married, I couldn't even coordinate the cooking times of the meat and vegetables I was preparing. I could burn meals better than any of the worst cooks around. Thankfully, I have a good, patient, and uncomplaining husband—and lucky for him I have improved a great deal!

It has been several years now since I have written most of this book. My youngest child is twenty-eight years old and we now have five grandchildren. Because of having to move from Maine, once again, more than four years ago to rural southwestern Pennsylvania due to my husband's work, the Lord has given me additional insight and lessons in home-making, thrift, and hospitality. My new neighborhood is mostly Amish. The Lord has allowed me to combine my sense of adventure and my love for homemaking. Now I can add my "empty nester" chapter to this book, allowing it to benefit women of any age. My hope is that women will glean new information that will prove helpful in their lives or at the very least, be entertained!

The Basics

It's important for me to note here that homemaking isn't just about cooking and keeping the house clean. It doesn't take a lot of money or perfection. It's a way you can show your family how much you love them by the way you care for them. Believe me, I'm not skilled in a lot of areas, but I have an interest in a lot of things. Unfortunately, this means I'm a "dabbler"—there are many things I like to do, but I never feel skilled in any one area. I do feel the Lord has been refining my skills over the years to share with others. Some friends have shared with me that they believe it is my gift from the Lord. My homemaking skills are all things that enable me to have the home atmosphere that I want for my family. We didn't own our own home until eleven years after we were married, but we tried to make each of the ten places we lived in comfortable, even though we didn't have a lot of money to spend.

One of the important things is to be somewhat organized. What I'm sharing is what I've learned along the way in homemaking, often learning by making mistakes. I'm also not always consistent in many things. I guess that's what makes me think I can help others, especially young moms that want to stay at home, but don't feel they can afford to.

Much of what I have to say is about the basics of feeding your family well and economically, and also maintaining your home. That is what I will concentrate on initially. This book is not about child rearing specifically, but about my passion for homemaking and all that it includes.

For eight years I shopped monthly for groceries and household items. That was certainly a time and money saver and it worked well for us during some of those busy years of child rearing. I'm not suggesting you do this, but I certainly learned a lot from it.

I guess I should start right at the basics of setting up your kitchen with the right tools and organizing your kitchen with what you have. If you don't have everything, you can look at the list and see how it applies to your needs. You can then start a list of your needs and wants, and prioritize. It has taken me more than thirty-six years to be able to say we have in our kitchen now not only our needs met, but most of our wants also. When we moved to Honduras in 1997, I had to start over to fill my house with the basics of home-making. We chose not to ship our household items to a third world country with a tropical climate and its problems, but to use what the shipping costs would be to fill the house with basic needs. I didn't realize that sometimes it is impossible to find some household items that I think are basic needs but are nonexistent in a third world country. Usually the cost was very high if I did want an item produced in the United States. I share this so you will understand that I do have recent experience in setting up a home from scratch.

Kitchen Basics

One of the gifts we received when we were married was Betty Crocker's *Dinner for Two Cookbook*. This book was a great help since it had a list of "what every kitchen for two needs." I didn't have everything on that list or the money to purchase the items, but it gave me a start and I was able to make a list of my needs. Sometimes I would purchase the item as I could afford or ask for it as a Christmas or birthday gift. Yard sales are a good source also. Besides the basics of a stove and refrigerator, a microwave oven now seems to be on most people's list. I obviously haven't always had one, however now that I do, I use mine regularly. Having a stand-alone freezer can certainly be a money saver, especially if you shop monthly or even every two weeks. If it is an old freezer that you inherited, it might be a time saver and convenience, but not a money saver.

Smaller items that are very useful are as follows:

- Electric coffee maker
- Toaster oven or toaster—Unplug when not in use.
- Food processor
- Blender
- Electric hand or stand mixer or both

- Slow cooker—I have several different sizes after thirty-six years.
- Wok—I prefer the non-electric type.
- Deep fryer or versatile hot pot—great for making chili or stews
- Electric griddle—Enables you to cook lots of pancakes, French toast, or toasted sandwiches at once. A non-electric would be less expensive.
- Pressure cooker—great for canning
- Electric waffle iron—The first one I had was purchased for a dollar at a yard sale.
- Kitchen scales—necessary especially if you buy in bulk and repackage food items
- Cake decorating bag and basic tubes—very useful and easy to learn how to use
- Wilton food coloring—Buy basic colors at first, then add to your collection as you can afford it. They will last for many years.
- Plastic and metal storage containers in a variety of sizes
- Spray bottles for homemade window cleaner, use recycled old spray bottles
- Window squeegee—saves time and paper towels
- Rubber spatulas—great for getting the last drop
- Wooden spoons—different sizes
- Masking tape—inexpensive and great for labeling containers for freezing
- Kitchen timer—I can time three things at once on mine. What busy mom couldn't use one? I've had mine for many years.
- Teakettle
- Ice bucket—great for parties and picnics
- Stainless steel pots and pans—Start with the basics and

add as you can afford and as your family grows. Include a double boiler in the basics or use a bowl over a pan of hot water.

•Baking pans—9"x13"; 8"x8"; 2 bread pans; cookie sheets; jellyroll pan; muffin tins; pizza pans; round 8" or 9" cake pans; a Bundt pan or tube pan; mini bread pans

•Colander—large and small

•Metal steam basket—fits into a saucepan to steam vegetables. Very inexpensive! A plastic steam basket made for the microwave works well also.

•Cake cooling racks

•Can opener—electric or hand operated

•Rolling pin

•Basting brush—helpful to have two

•Pasta fork—very inexpensive

•Wire whisk—helpful to have several in different sizes and a Teflon coated whisk for nonstick pans

•Salad forks or tongs—Mine were given to me by a local department store for signing their bridal registry over thirty-six years ago.

•Metal tongs

•Pancake turners—metal and plastic for nonstick pans

•Vegetable peeler

•Kitchen scissors—the type you can use to cut poultry

•Funnels—various sizes

•Large roast forks—helpful to remove large roasts or poultry from a pan

•Graters or shredders—Works great for small amounts of foods, especially good if you don't have a food processor.

•Long-handled slotted spoon

•Vegetable brush

- Knives—best you can afford in a variety of sizes. At least two paring knives.
- Long-handled soup ladle
- Stainless steel flatware—Start with service for eight, although twelve would be better. Also, serving pieces are useful.
- Long-handled masher
- Measuring cups—two sets are great, dry and liquid
- Measuring spoons—two sets are great here as well
- Glass measuring bowls—basics at first, several sizes are nice but not necessary
- Set of mixing bowls—Pyrex bowls can be used in the microwave oven and conventional oven.
- Casserole dishes—various sizes with covers
- Large salad bowl
- Pizza cutter
- Garlic press—a luxury but not necessary
- Pastry blender
- Ice cream scoop—metal, large for ice cream, medium for cookie dough, and small for melon balls. The better the quality, the longer it will last.
- Meat thermometer—I like the instant read.
- Steak knives
- Flour sifter—If you buy flour in bulk always sift your flour, especially if you use unbleached.
- Pie plates—8-, 9-, and 10-inch sizes
- Food mill—great for making applesauce and pureeing foods for a baby
- Baskets—various sizes. Great to use for bread, napkins, flatware, or to hold anything!
- Cutting boards—can use as a trivet also!
- Trivets—These don't have to be expensive, but it's nice if they are decorative.

•Punch bowl—very helpful over the years, and doesn't have to be expensive

•Apple peeler/corer—Watch for sales or check yard sales. Very helpful to prepare apples for freezing and works quickly. Mine is a clamp-on type, although a suction base would work better.

•Serving trays—different sizes for serving snacks to guests in and outside. Not necessary, but a nice touch!

•Mesh strainer—use for dusting cakes, etc. You can get these in different sizes, inexpensively.

•Jell-O molds—One basic size is sufficient. Also, Popsicle molds are helpful if you have children.

•Knife sharpener—small type is very useful

•Frying pans—choose nonstick or cast iron. I prefer nonstick for most cooking.

•Cake pedestal—makes a simple cake look special

•Drinking glasses—I keep the basics in my cupboard for every day. Years ago I bought a set of clear, inexpensive drinking glasses to use when we had guests. I kept them stored in a box for those special occasions when I wanted matched glasses.

•Bread machine—I have had one for many years, and it's one of my favorite small appliances. It's really a luxury though, not a need. I often use it to mix pizza dough. It's so easy to roll out after it has been mixed in the bread machine.

All of these tools aren't absolutely necessary, but very helpful. I'm sure there are many other items I could list, but these are the basics.

Kitchen Setup

Set up your kitchen in a way that everything is placed in an area near where it will be used. For example, potholders should be kept near the stove. Spices should be near your food preparation area. Plates, flatware, and napkins should be placed close to the eating area. Drinking glasses should be placed near the drinking water source. We have a closet in our kitchen in Maine, so I had my husband change the setup so I had a smaller area to hang up coats and an area with shelves to use as a pantry. That still leaves me room to store my ironing board, iron, a large container of flour, as well as a broom, dustpan, feather duster, and boots.

On my kitchen counters I keep a few small appliances, canister set, knife set, breadbox, and kitchen utensil jar. Everything else on my counter I would consider clutter. An easy way to prevent clutter in your home is to pick up after yourself and teach it to the rest of your family by example. The key to this is to make sure the house is in order before you go to bed each night so you have a good start in the morning. If things are put back in the appropriate place after use, you won't have that to do at bedtime. I worked three days a week while my children were growing up so I know this works well, even if you have a very busy life.

Keep sharp instruments and anything that could be harmful to children out of reach. Always keep pot handles that are in use on the stove away from where a child could reach it. A pastor's wife in Virginia, who we were visiting at the time, gave me a great timesaving tip many years ago. She suggested I tape my most frequently used recipes on the inside of my cupboard near the food preparation area. This has been such a great help over the years. For me, I placed my piecrust recipe, my imitation maple syrup recipe, and my brown sugar and confectioners' sugar measurement conversion charts just inside my cupboards.

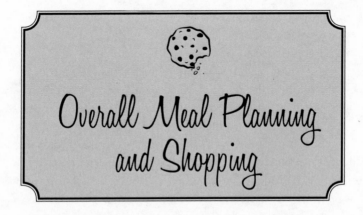

Overall Meal Planning and Shopping

Years ago, I tried to make grocery and household item planning as quick and easy as possible. For me that meant I needed to come up with a master list. Before doing my shopping, I would run down my master list and add to my shopping list any items I was low on or out of. I have always purchased very few packaged mixes or convenience foods unless they were an exceptional value in either time or money, as opposed to "from scratch" food items. This makes the basic master list much easier, especially if you buy in bulk.

Ideally, you should make a two-week or a month's list of menus, depending on how often you shop. This has not worked well for me. When the kids were very small perhaps it would have worked, however I was too naïve to know I should make one. During the busy teen years, being a taxi for the kids and their friends, church responsibilities, and my work forced me to be flexible with meal planning. Also, I never knew how many people would be at home to eat. My way of replenishing foods on my master list and having tried and true recipes available allowed me to be flexible whether we had four or seven at the table at mealtime.

I always decide what we will have for supper either the night before or in the morning. I take what I need from the freezer, find the recipe I will be using and place it on the counter in the food preparation area. Make sure you thaw your frozen meat in the refrigerator. If it is a large roast or turkey, it obviously won't be thawed by early afternoon that day or even the next. You need to plan ahead for large items. Have a general plan for every meal. Think color, texture, nutritional value, and cost. An example of planning a colorful meal might be choosing a colorful vegetable, such as peas or green beans, to go with mashed potatoes and roasted chicken. You could serve sweet potato instead of white potato to add color. An example of texture might include a crunchy coating on oven-fried chicken, if serving with mashed potatoes and squash. Adding a salad adds texture and fiber also. I always try to make sure to serve at least three combinations at the supper meal. First, use a protein source such as meat, pork, poultry, or fish. You could also use tofu, beans, lentils, etc. Second, add a starch such as potato, pasta, or rice. Third, include one or more frozen or fresh vegetable, cooked or raw. Often it would be a cooked frozen vegetable with a salad. If you prefer casseroles, make sure the casserole contains protein, vegetables, and a starch or supplement the casserole with a side dish that completes the meal. Involve the kids in food preparation, as they are able, especially if you work outside the home. It's good training.

A friend once told me that she writes on a small calendar what she has served each night for the evening or large meal of the day. This way she could use it as a quick reference when pressed for time. This worked well for me during my busiest years and is interesting to look back on now. Her suggestion was to pick up a free pocket-sized calendar at the end of each year, which you could keep on top of a recipe box for quick entries and reference.

I want to discuss thriftiness out of need, since this is a focus of this book. When my husband and I were first married we started on a tight budget while he went back to college to get his bachelor's degree. Our first child, Chris, was due shortly after our first wedding anniversary. Many times we had to be thrifty, but I know now that they were learning and character-building years. We have great compassion for others going through those stages in their lives. Another thrifty friend of mine once told me that it's not all bad to be financially strapped as a housewife and mom because it encourages you to be creative. That is also true from my experience! Paul tells us in Philippians 4:12, "I know what it is to be in need, and I know what it is to have plenty. I have learned the secret of being content in any and every situation, whether well fed or hungry, whether living in plenty or in want." Being creative and generous with what the Lord has provided and being thankful is a lesson well learned!

If I narrowed my shopping to exactly what each recipe called for on a menu plan I probably could have saved more, but I would have been less flexible to share with our friends through hospitality. Also, several years ago we had an exchange student from Bangkok, Thailand live with us for six months. It was a wonderful experience, but very busy with three teenagers in the house and my oldest son home from college on weekends. However, adjusting my meal planning to include another person was not difficult since I restocked the basics on my master list with each regular shopping trip.

Following this chapter is a sample of my master list. You do not need to copy it, but I encourage you to use it as a guide as you establish your own. During the eight years that I shopped monthly, Sam's Club and Wal-Mart were not available in our rural area. We lived about a half-hour's drive from the nearest supermarket and an hour from the nearest shopping mall. Also, my intent is not to spend long hours in the kitchen cooking complicated and time-consuming dishes. Although I enjoyed cooking, usually I didn't have a lot of time.

I confess I'm not a morning person by design and have a difficult time facing food early in the morning. Breakfast on weekday mornings in our house included simple, quick foods such as toast, English muffins, unsweetened cereal, juice, milk, microwave pancakes, or French toast (saved and frozen from extra made on the weekends), and fruit in season. On the weekends I could handle pancakes, French toast, eggs, or omelets if I could make them later than 7:30 a.m.! My husband, Steve, was often our weekend cook. When trying to save money on breakfast foods, I have found that buying cold cereals, especially sweetened cereals, are not a good value for your money. I would buy the basic lower-priced cereals such as Cheerios, Corn Flakes, Rice Krispies, Kix, etc. and allow one large bowl each, supplementing if they were still hungry with toast or English muffins. Sometimes the kids would want oatmeal, the basic quick oats that I would buy in bulk from the health food store, cooked for 1 ½ minutes (per 1 cup serving), in the microwave. See the recipe section for cooking old-fashioned oatmeal in the microwave in 3 minutes, which is even more nutritious.

I made the lunches for school and work the night before. Sometimes the kids bought hot lunches, depending on the child and the amount of money in the budget that week. Their beverage was usually milk from school. When a drink was needed for afternoon sports, I would freeze juice, water, or iced tea in a reusable freezer container the night before and wrapped it well in a paper towel before putting it in their reusable lunch bag in the morning. For fruit or snacks such as crackers, chips, raisins, and pretzels, I would buy the large packages and place individual portions in sandwich bags, appropriately freezing or storing the remainder to last until my next shopping trip. Items such as crackers, chips, pretzels, etc. can be frozen to keep them fresh.

Afternoon snacks were often leftovers, cookies (home-made only, since one of my favorite things to do is to bake homemade cookies), popcorn, pretzels, or cheese and crack-ers. Sometimes I would give them graham crackers with a few chocolate chips and a teaspoon of marshmallow fluff between them that I had microwaved a few seconds. This is kind of like a s'more. Honestly, they almost never wanted fruit for a snack while they were teenagers.

For meal ideas when we had company coming (other than the kids' friends), I kept index cards in the front of my recipe file box containing a different guest meal on each card. It listed different menu suggestions and where to find the rec-ipe. This way I didn't have to stop and figure out what went well with a ham meal, for example. I also had two seperate cards listing several good and simple dessert ideas. According to what I had on hand, I could make my choice and easily find the recipe. I also had a card listing likes and dislikes of people, such as missionaries, to use as a reference, since they might not visit again for several years. If I had to think the whole meal through each time, I would probably not have invited guests in so often. The cards did not take very long to setup, and were easy enough to do while watching TV in the evening! I encourage Christian families to invite missionar-ies and speakers that occasionally visit your church to a meal or to stay overnight. This is such a blessing and education for your children. It's not necessary to have a guestroom or lots of money; use what you have, be creative, and you won't regret it!

In the summer months I tried to include the kids on my shopping trips. I know this does not seem like it would be economical. Usually I hear and read that it is not wise to take children grocery shopping because it costs you more, but I disagree. It was especially helpful during the years that I shopped monthly. They got an education in economical shopping and I got to enjoy their company and assistance. We started the day off with a good breakfast and then went on our shopping adventure. We chose that one day a month to go to a fast food restaurant for lunch. We could have taken a bag lunch and had a picnic if there wasn't enough money to eat out; however this was a time to treat the kids for their help. While shopping, they would help with the calculator and we would discuss why I chose one product over another. They could compare costs and know firsthand what empty calories cost. All three children have learned how to compare unit prices, budget, and check for nutritional value. This also gave them a chance to help with meal planning. Often if they wanted to try a high-priced convenience food we would figure out how we could make it from scratch, cheaper and better. When Chris was in high school he had a love for a local restaurant's chicken cordon bleu. I think we came up with a homemade version that was very similar and afford-able for all of us to enjoy at home.

Some of the other homemade versions we have enjoyed over the years are a substitute for Bisquick, rice mixes, deep dish and fresh dough pizza, cookie ice cream sandwiches, pancake syrup, and large deli-type sub sandwiches using loaves of Italian or French bread. It does take discipline to shop from your list and not pick up items that catch your eye. If you see an item that you would really like to try, work it into your list the next time you shop. Packaged, processed, empty calorie foods were occasionally requested by my kids, but rarely purchased. I would tell them they needed to have something to look forward to when they were grown and on their own. Items such as canned spaghetti and meatballs, TV dinners, packaged cookies, etc., were what they usually wanted because they would see the ads on TV or in magazines. When Chris was in college and had his first apartment, he did have those food items, but I think he got tired of them quite quickly! He seemed to enjoy coming home to his old favorites.

My husband and children, especially the boys, have never been light eaters. They were rugged males with healthy appetites. I'm the shortest in our family at 5' 8"! I heard Stacy, my daughter-in-law, say several years ago that she didn't see how I fed my family economically when they were all home since they were such hearty eaters.

We have always had a garden in the summer, but not a particularly large one. I was primarily the only one who enjoyed working in the garden, but I worked out of the home part-time so I had only a limited amount of time. A garden can be a real money saver, though. I canned a year's worth of string beans and tomatoes, and froze corn, snow peas, green peppers, and beets. I also made pickles and relishes. I have an especially good hot dog relish that I make yearly. I make applesauce in the fall, as well as freezing apples. I now have two of my own apple trees that supply me with enough good eating apples for my family and friends. I usually have enough left over to freeze or use for applesauce and desserts. We pick strawberries and raspberries in season to freeze, eat fresh, and use in jams. I buy Maine blueberries in twenty-pound flats when they are in season to eat fresh, freeze, and share with friends and family. Vary your meal planning according to the availability of seasonal foods and food on sale.

To help get meals on the table more quickly, all three kids had a job to do. They were responsible for setting the table at suppertime, as they became old enough. Initially, I had a problem getting them to do their part without a lot of coaxing. We finally had to say that the table was to be set at five p.m. If the table was not set by the time the meal was to be served then they would have to wait to start until Steve and I had finished eating. Also, each one had to have done his/ her part or all of the kids would have to wait. This encouraged teamwork. There were very few times when the kids had to wait to eat until after we had finished and I didn't have to spend my time arguing with them to do their job. This worked well for the years the kids were all home and not involved in sports during the evening mealtime. In my experience, children need to know that your "yes" means yes and your "no" means no. This way they clearly know their boundaries. However, leave room to discuss a quick decision that you made that might not have been a fair one, but one made in anger.

We have always made a point of sitting at the table together for the evening meal. Those days went by so fast that I'm glad that we had that time together as a family. When Chris was involved in high school football, he had to miss most weekly evening meals with the rest of us. I remember once that he said the one thing he missed during football season was that time together as a family at suppertime.

For a while, we had one night a week that the kids could invite a friend for supper. That night was often pizza night, since it was popular with kids and an easy meal to expand economically. However, if someone extra was at our home any night they were welcome to share the meal with us.

Sometimes using stemmed glassware and cloth napkins make an ordinary meal special. Even if it was just Steve and I, (which it often is now), nice napkins, dinnerware, and candles can make the meal special. An instrumental CD playing softly is also a nice touch. These extras don't cost a lot, but show your family that you value the time with them and also gives you an excellent opportunity to teach them and allow them to practice table manners and etiquette.

When meal planning, one of the newer trends is to try once a month cooking, which I have not done. Often our meals are not time consuming in preparation anyway and I actually like getting a meal. It's not unusual for me to make two casseroles at one time and freeze one for later. Usually I do this with lasagna because it can be time intensive and makes a lot of dirty dishes! I might feel burdened knowing I would have an intensive cooking day every two weeks or once monthly, but that is just my preference. I preferred to spend my time during weekends that I didn't have to work with my family rather than in the kitchen.

Perhaps you never had a meal plan or a master grocery list. You might want to start writing down what you are serving for meals and start saving all of your grocery receipts for a month or so. Even save receipts from those quick stops at convenience stores. If it's a typical month, you should be able to see where your money goes and if you have eaten out more than your budget allows. You can also see what the quality of your meals are. From the past months' menus and grocery receipts you will be able to tell which food and household items you use regularly, how much you use, and begin to compile a master list. Now if I were a more disciplined organizer (and maybe I will be someday), I would tell you to set up your master list according to the way the aisles are set up in the grocery store where you shop. My sister once told me that she used to set up her grocery list in that way, but she is much more organized than I am. I do list the different items under the particular store where I usually purchase them, such as the meats at the meat market, bread at the bakery thrift outlet, spices, oatmeal, flour, etc. at the health food store. I also list the stores in the sequence that I need to stop at in order to save time and gas. Remember to take a cooler during warm weather to keep foods that need to be kept cold from spoiling. Try to shop for perishables and frozen foods last.

I remember some months when I didn't have the money to get all of what I thought our needs were. Be creative; trust the Lord to guide you. Bible verses that have been very helpful to me are Matthew 6:19–34, and also always hold onto God's promise in Matthew 6:33 and 34, especially where Jesus says, "But seek first His kingdom and His righteousness, and all these things will be given to you as well. Therefore do not worry about tomorrow, for tomorrow will worry about itself. Each day has enough trouble of its own."

Don't just expect the Lord to meet your needs without "seeking first the kingdom of God and His righteousness." Have a good sense of humor and remember what a friend told me once: "Dwell on what you do have, not on what you don't have." Treat your meal planning and shopping as a challenge and tackle the jobs in a creative way!

I have had mothers ask how I keep my family from eating all of the "good stuff" up before the month's end. One example is to not let the kids sit and eat a half box of cereal for breakfast. One bowl plus toast or whatever else is available is sufficient. If they did eat it up within a few days, it would not be available until the next shopping trip. I buy very few packaged products such as cookies and snacks and I keep items such as chocolate chips in the freezer (to keep me out of them more so than the kids). An American friend in Honduras said that she wrapped her bags of chocolate chips in aluminum foil and labeled them "liver" before placing them in the freezer. She never had a problem with her family getting into them! Chocolate chips are a valuable item to an American chocoholic living in a third world country! I put labels on foods that I wanted saved for a special occasion and the kids honored that. My kids became very good about asking if it was okay to eat or finish certain foods since I was so careful about the food purchases I made.

The Master List

I keep my master list in the same notebook that I use to store all of my other important information such as birthdays, Christmas lists, family sizes, goals, etc. It's a very inexpensive 5" x 8" size loose-leaf notebook that I can throw in my suitcase when traveling. I have used riding time to start a grocery list or work on my Christmas gift-planning list on the way home from a vacation.

My master list is not in any special order, as I've stated previously, nor is it an all-inclusive list. However, it is a good representation of what I use in my home.

Yogurt
Eggs or substitute
Fresh fruits
Fresh vegetables
Cereal
Vanilla extract
Flour
Stuffing mix
Sugar–White
Sugar–Brown
Confectioners' sugar
Pudding mix

Shortening
Canola oil
Olive oil
Nonstick cooking spray
Sea salt
Pepper
Baking soda
Baking powder
Spices
Coffee
Tea
Iced tea mix
Hot chocolate mix
Mustard
Relish
Ketchup
Honey
Peanut butter
Canned soups
Rice
BBQ sauce
Tomato paste
Maple flavoring
Pasta
Pasta sauce
Potatoes
Noodles
Cocoa
Powdered milk
Evaporated milk
Red wine vinegar
White vinegar
Apple cider vinegar

Soy sauce
Worcestershire sauce
Jell-O
Beef
Poultry
Fish
Pork or ham
Hot dogs
Canned tuna, clams
Luncheon meats
Mayonnaise
Cheese—Cheddar, American, Mozzarella, Swiss,
    Parmesan
Cream cheese
Sour cream
Pepperoni
Canned pineapple
Yeast
Chocolate chips
Oatmeal
Crackers
Nacho chips
Pretzels
Margarine
Milk
Kool-Aid
Canned vegetables
Raisins
Marshmallows
Pimentos
Salad dressings
Sure gel
Juice

Ice cream
Bread
Napkins
Make-up
Aluminum foil
Plastic wrap
Waxed paper
Zip lock bags—Pint, quart, gallon, sandwich
Body lotion
Rubbing alcohol
Vitamins
Personal care products
Soap
Dishwasher soap
Detergent
Fabric softener
Ammonia
Bleach
Liquid soap
Toilet tissue
Tissues
Paper towels
Cat food
Cat litter
Milk
Soda
Bean sprouts
Chow mein noodles
Water chestnuts
Wonton or egg roll wrappers
Bathroom cleaner
Toilet bowl cleaner
Q-tips

Trash bags
Disposable razors
Antiperspirant
Antacids
Tylenol
Ibuprofen
Contact lens solutions
Toothpaste
RX medications
Cotton balls
Non-chlorine bleach
Windshield washer fluid

Some items that would not have been included on my master list back in the days that the kids were being raised were: Bisquick, croutons, breadcrumbs, sweetened cereal, pancake syrup, unsweetened chocolate, and sweetened condensed milk. I'm sure there were more; however these were the ones that I usually omitted because I had a better or less expensive homemade substitute. Stuffing mix is one item that I did include on my list because I found a packaged product that we liked much better than any I made myself. I make my own pizza sauce, but prefer the purchased spaghetti sauce, mainly because it's quick. Since I use it very seldom it is often cheaper than making a large batch of spaghetti sauce from scratch, considering the time and electricity it takes to cook it for a long period of time. The exception would probably be if I grew most of the ingredients and needed to use them up. In my next chapter, I will go into more detail regarding some items on my master list.

As the kids were old enough, they knew when they needed certain items such as socks, underwear, deodorant, pens, notebooks, etc. They were usually good about adding their needs to the grocery list, which is a running list that I kept in a kitchen drawer. The rule was that if you used something up or saw that we were low on something, it was your job to add it to the list at that time. I don't have a great memory so I need to write things down as I see the need and a month can be a long time to remember what that need was. You will notice that I include a lot of items in my grocery/household budget category. It was often challenging to fit it all into the budget, but we usually succeeded.

Years ago I was curious to learn how my grocery budget compared to that of the government food stamp program, so I called the Department of Health and Welfare to compare. I don't recall the exact numbers now, but I know as best as they could figure out, their food stamp allowance per person was greater than what I was spending. Not only was I shopping well on a budget, I was secure knowing that my family was getting balanced, nutritious meals. As I viewed various mothers in the checkout lines at the supermarket, I could see that many families needed more education on how to feed their families nutritiously and economically. If I can help just one of those moms feed her family more responsibly, it will be worth all the time I have spent on this book.

More About My Master List

Assuming you have saved your grocery lists, menus, and receipts for a couple of weeks or months and checked what items you keep stocked, you should be able to write your own master list. You should now know what it costs for most of the items on your list. If you're not sure, take time to visit the store where you shop regularly as well as stores nearby to compare quality, cost, and convenience. Be sure to check newspaper flyers for sales and plan your menus around the sales. Try the warehouse stores, but be careful to compare prices. Sometimes a generic or store brand item in a supermarket or health food store might be cheaper and just as good as the brand name product at a wholesale shopping club. I can buy very good unbleached flour in a fifty-pound bag at a local health food store much cheaper than I ever see in any other store. I like the best quality I can find at the best price; however, plan your stops so that you don't spend more on gas to save a nickel somewhere else. I know I can get 90% lean ground beef at a shopping club cheaper than I can get it at the local supermarkets (unless the supermarket has a good sale), so I plan to go there once a month to buy it in bulk. I know of other products I use regularly that I can also find in bulk there, so I plan those purchases at the same time. If the best price you can find is in a larger size than you can afford, or is in a larger size than you can use in a reasonable amount of time, ask a relative, friend, or group of friends to split the product with you, including the cost. Also make sure to store large amounts properly. I tend not to buy large amounts of flour in the summer because the plastic container that I have to hold a fifty-pound bag of flour is not as tight fitting as I would like, and I have gotten bugs in my flour. I just *hate* bugs in my kitchen! Even during the colder months I put bay leaves in my flour container to prevent bugs. I also always sift my flour for that reason. A friend once told me that bugs don't seem to bother the bleached flour because there's not the nutritive value in it that unbleached flour has. I prefer the unbleached for my family!

Be sure to check unit prices in the supermarkets, since the largest container isn't always the best value. Supermarkets, warehouse shopping clubs, and health food stores aren't always the cheapest stores to shop. Consider liquidation warehouses, bakery thrift shops, and occasionally convenience stores. I used to drive by one convenience store all the time that always advertised lower prices on luncheon meats, potatoes, and bananas, as well as various other food products, well below the price I had found those items locally in other stores. I tried the quality and it was very good. The products are considered loss leaders that get you into the store hoping you will purchase other products as well. I like to be ethical in these cases, though, and give the store my business for other things when I can. In this instance, I would also buy gasoline there.

When I was raising my family, canned soups seemed to be reasonably priced. Now I find they are very expensive. If I were raising a family now as a stay-at-home mom, I would try experimenting with making my own versions of cream of celery, cream of mushroom, or cream of chicken soup. Start with a basic cream sauce and add lightly sautéed celery, sautéed or canned mushrooms, or leftover bits of chicken and broth. With the Internet now it would be very easy to find a recipe that someone else has already developed.

Meats

When shopping for meats do your homework and know the prices at the supermarkets close to you and check the weekly sales flyers. You don't have to get the most expensive cuts of meat. Often the most expensive cuts are well marbled, meaning there is fat throughout the meat, which tenderizes and flavors it. You can shop for less expensive, less marbled cuts of beef such as London broil or flank steak, which need to be sliced thin against the grain after cooking. If you marinate the meat for at least one hour before cooking, you will add flavor and tenderize it. I have some very basic marinade recipes for both chicken and beef.

Roasts are also often on sale. Buy the largest you can afford and divide it into meal portions. If you freeze it slightly, it will slice much easier. Using a very sharp knife, cut a portion off to use as a roast, then thinly slice portions for minute steak sandwiches and/or stir-fry, cube for kabobs (marinate if used for kabobs) or stew beef.

Ground Beef

Ninety percent ground beef is my choice since it is lower in fat. For grilled hamburgers I often use 80% lean, which seems to make a moister hamburger or use the 90% and add water to the burger gently forming it with my hands. Often I have to buy 90% ground round in six to ten-pound packages to get the best price. I repackage the meat into the size packages I will be using. I make hamburger patties out of some of the ground beef. I spray cookie sheets lightly with nonstick cooking spray before placing the patties on them and covering with plastic wrap. Then I place the cookie sheets in the freezer only long enough to freeze the hamburgers. Once frozen, I store the hamburgers in freezer bags or recycled plastic freezer containers. There were times that I didn't feel I wanted or could afford to spend my food money for freezer bags. In fact I seldom did, instead using recycled plastic containers for freezing. I have also made meatballs in four-pound batches, browned them on greased cookie sheets in the oven, and frozen them in meal-size portions. They can be used in a variety of ways, such as spaghetti and meatballs, barbecue meatballs, sweet and sour meatballs, Swedish meatballs, or in meatball subs.

To say a little more about the use of zipper type freezer bags, I should add that I really like the convenience that they offer when used for marinating and freezing meats and vegetables; however, the same tasks can be done just as easily in a more cost-efficient way. Marinating can be done in a plastic or glass dish. I used to buy new plastic bread bags by the roll in bakery thrift outlets. For freezing foods I would double bag them, making sure to remove all of the air before sealing to prevent freezer burn. I saved whipped topping containers, margarine tubs, marshmallow fluff containers, etc. to freeze meats, vegetables, and fruits in. They are reusable and a great way to recycle.

Pork

Pork is meat that I didn't purchase a lot because it contained so much fat; however, now pork is much leaner. Watch for sales and buy the largest size roast you can afford. If it is bone-in, you can cut up some of it into pork chops. Boneless pork roasts are sometimes inexpensive in the shopping club store. You can leave some as a roast, slice some into steaks, thinly slice for stir-fry, or cube before repackaging and freezing in meal size portions. Usually I ask someone in the meat department to slice or cut up the meat for me while I continue to shop. The shopping club chain that I belong to does this as a free service. This can be a great time-saving convenience.

Ham

My family used to enjoy ham, which is much leaner these days than when I was raising my family. I would often buy the largest canned ham I could find on sale or the largest rolled ham on sale. Ham is a very versatile meat. You can slice it for grilling, cube it for casseroles and omelets, and/or leave part of it in a large piece for baking with a brown sugar and pineapple glaze. Make sure you know whether your ham is completely cooked or needs cooking. If it is not previously cooked, cook as directed and then divide it as you like. The previously cooked ham can be sliced for sandwiches, including homemade English muffin sandwiches for breakfast with cooked egg and cheese, or cold sliced in the summer to serve with a potato salad. I have had great success freezing previously cooked ham. The shopping club that I shop at will cut up the precooked hams I purchase. I have them thin slice a portion for sandwiches, thick slice some for grilling and leave the rest in a large chunk for baking, cubing, etc.

Poultry

We really like poultry and since it is low fat and versatile, we tend to eat a lot of it. If I find a small inexpensive whole chicken, I cut it in half or quarters for grilling or baking. A quick and easy way to bake cut-up chicken is to marinate it for at least an hour but not more than twenty-four hours. Mix up some stuffing; using an ice cream scoop, place a mound of stuffing on a greased baking pan. Cover with a quartered piece of chicken and bake at 350 degrees until done, about 50 minutes. Just make sure you don't overcook, because the chicken will become dry. If you don't have time to marinate the chicken, brush with barbecue sauce. Cooking baked potatoes at the same time also works well, but remember that you might need to put the potatoes into the oven about fifteen minutes before the chicken, depending on the size of the potatoes.

Look for large chickens or turkeys on sale, even though your family might be small. Large whole chickens or turkey make good company meals and the leftovers can be frozen in meal-sized packages for later use. I freeze two-cup packages of cooked, cut-up chicken or turkey for later use in casseroles, salads, stir fry, or sandwiches. This way you don't have to eat poultry for several days in a row! After taking the cooked poultry off the bone, you can use the carcass to make a tasty chicken soup or chicken stock (a chicken soup recipe made from a carcass can be found in my recipe section). Recently I have heard that cooking the poultry carcass again to make soup stock causes the bone marrow to break down, thus causing a bitter taste. I have not had that problem with the recipe I use.

Buy the cut you can afford at the best price. Thighs are usually the highest ratio of meat to bone in cut up poultry, but not the leanest. Chicken breasts are about a 50% yield of meat to bone, as I understand it. I've found that if you can find boneless, skinless chicken breast or thighs on sale you not only save money, but time as well. Usually you will find the best sale-priced poultry in large, family-sized packages. I've noticed that boneless, skinless chicken breasts are often on sale at a very good price now due to their popularity. This was not the case, however, when we were raising our family.

Hot Dogs

Although hot dogs are not very low fat or nutritious, they sure are tasty! I tried not to serve them more than twice a month to my family. On some of those busy game nights years ago we ate what was quick and easy. Hot dogs fell into that category! Often meat markets or shopping clubs sell hotdogs in large-sized packages. The meat market I used to shop while raising my family would have large-sized packages of hotdogs that were considered seconds, which meant they were irregular in size. For the savings we received on these quality, good-tasting hotdogs, we didn't have a problem if the hot dogs weren't all a uniform size. In shopping clubs, if a product is nearing its expiration date it is often marked way down to get rid of it before it expires. I take the item home, repackage in meal-serving sizes and freeze. I can almost always find at least one exceptional buy on a product at the shopping club that I frequent. Be alert for their markdowns!

When repackaging foods, especially for freezing, remember not to refreeze meats unless you cook first. Wrap tightly or store in a container that leaves the least amount of air in the package. Label well with the date, contents, and amount. I find that masking tape works well for labeling packages, as it is inexpensive and removes easily on plastic containers. I like a fine point Sharpie permanent marker for writing on the tape.

Eggs

Consider eggs a good value when planning meals. Eggs are not just for breakfast or baking. They keep well when stored in the carton for at least three weeks in the refrigerator. While living in Central America we bought eggs placed in plastic bags from a table at the front of the grocery store. They never refrigerated them. We never became ill; however, they were well cooked before I served them. I don't recommend this storage method, though! I believe that eating eggs in moderation is not unhealthy unless your doctor has found that you have a dangerously high cholesterol level. We enjoy quiche for an evening meal. You can use up leftover vegetables, meats, and cheeses in a quiche and it's easy to put together. When our kids were quite young, I worked one evening a week, which left that meal up to my husband. Their childhood memories of those evenings included scrambled eggs, ham or sausage, and toast cooked for them by their dad. Sarah said that was a good bonding night!

Fresh Fruit

Buying fruits in season or on sale is the most economical way to shop. Know where you can purchase the fruit that your family enjoys at the lowest price. Remember that convenience store that I mentioned earlier that always seemed to have bananas on sale at a good price?

If you can find fresh berries in the summer at a reasonable price, buy all that you can afford. Eat the berries fresh, freeze, or make jam with the rest in the amounts that you can use within a year until the next berry season arrives. Often the least expensive way to purchase berries is to pick them yourself. Check the classified ad section of the newspaper when berries and fruit are in season. Get your children to help you pick them if age appropriate. Canning is also a good way to preserve foods, but you must follow canning instructions exactly to ensure a safe and quality product and protect yourself from serious burns.

My Aunt Pearl and I made an annual event in July of going to buy our "flat" of blueberries in a small town near the coast of Maine. Other than this outing, we don't seem to have a lot of time together. This time was special over the years. In Maine, we seem to be more limited in the fresh fruits we can buy locally grown. Apples, raspberries, black-berries, strawberries, and pears are the commonly grown Maine fruits. The fresh fruit season is short in the North, but in the mountains of southwestern Pennsylvania the growing seasons, although similar to Maine's, produce peaches, pears, grapes, and early apples. Berries freeze well on cookie sheets when placed in a single layer. I don't wash fresh berries before freezing because this causes them to stick together. Once frozen, place in freezer bags or containers and they will remain separated. You can then take out the amount needed for a particular recipe or for eating without having to thaw the whole container. Wash them in a colander under warm water just before using. Don't pick berries after a rain shower because they will absorb the water and become mushy, I learned this the hard way!

Some supermarkets mark down bruised and over ripe fruits and vegetables on certain days of the week. Ask the produce manager in the supermarkets that you frequent to find out what they do. Whether you have the over ripe fruits in your house or purchase them inexpensively, there are many recipes you can use them in. For example, bananas can be used in banana bread, cake, or smoothies. If you only have one banana that is over ripe, peel it and place it in a freezer bag or container and freeze until you have collected enough to use in baking. Over ripe or bruised apples can be used in desserts, applesauce, muffins, etc., depending on how many you have. If you have quite a few apples that have bruises or bad areas make applesauce. Wash, core, quarter, remove the bad area (but don't peel the whole apple) then place in a large microwavable bowl, cover the bowl with a piece of waxed paper to prevent splashing while cooking. Microwave on high for about ten or fifteen minutes, stirring with a wooden spoon at three to four-minute intervals. When the apples seem soft, place them in a food mill or sieve to strain and remove the peels. The type of apple will determine the cooking time for the applesauce. I like to make my applesauce this way because it uses the least amount of cooking time and the applesauce retains more of the pink color. I don't dry the apples after I wash them before cooking and I add only about ⅛ cup of water, which is less water than you would need if you were going to cook them on the stove. This is a great way to make applesauce when you don't have a lot of time or don't want to have to dirty pots and pans. I just rinse the bowl, then throw into the dishwasher to clean.

Fruit juices seem to be less expensive when you buy at least the twelve-ounce frozen concentrate size container. Try different brands; some store brands are equally as tasty as brand names and are much less expensive. I once tried diluting the orange juice a little more than the directions called for to stretch into more servings, but my family quickly noticed the difference. If you have leftover pineapple juice from using canned pineapple in another recipe, pour the leftover juice together with your orange juice.

Fresh Vegetables

Buy fresh vegetables according to what is on sale or in season, or grow them yourself, and plan your meals accordingly. For example, in Maine fresh peas are only available at a good price in late June or early July. We like peas so I keep the store brand frozen petite peas on hand. Often the larger package is the most economical, but not always. Fresh cabbage is often cheapest in season or in March around St. Patrick's Day. This is a good time to pull out your cabbage recipes. Try different types of lettuce according to what is on sale. Try growing your own herbs in the summertime and dry, or grow inside in pots if you have time to tend them during the winter months.

Recently I started roasting some fresh vegetables in the oven in some olive oil and sprinkling with sea salt and fresh ground pepper. I roast them for about twenty minutes at 400 to 425 degrees, depending on the vegetable. This change in cooking some vegetables has given me a whole new love and enjoyment for them. Try it! I enjoy roasted green beans, asparagus, broccoli, potatoes, carrots, and sweet potatoes. A little olive oil is better for you than butter.

Cereal

As I have mentioned before, this area can really throw off your food budget. Many cold cereals are high priced and loaded with sugar. I did not buy sweetened cereal in those early years of raising my family. Every month, I bought three or four large boxes of different kinds of the unsweetened

Jean Clark

cereal, as well as having oatmeal available. I continue to buy my oatmeal (quick oats) in bulk at the health food store. Regular oatmeal is even more nutritious and inexpensive in bulk at the health food store. By bulk, I don't mean in a fifty-pound bag, but that is even less expensive if you can use it up, store it properly, or share the cost with several friends. Quick oatmeal can be quickly cooked in the microwave in the bowl you will be eating from. If you want maple-flavored with brown sugar, just add maple flavoring and top with a little brown sugar before serving. Stay away from the color-ful packaged oatmeal in nice little individual packages. It's nearly as quick from scratch and much cheaper. By buying the generic cold cereals such as the flaked corn or crisp rice, you can use them in cooking also, such as desserts, coatings for chicken, or for adding to meatballs, etc. As I have said previously, I didn't give my kids the option to have several bowls of cereal for breakfast, but gave them toast, English muffins, or homemade muffins or English muffin bread along with their cereal.

Flour

As I've mentioned earlier, I buy a good quality of unbleached flour in a fifty-pound bag at my favorite health food store. It is a good investment to buy good containers to store the flour in. If you use whole-wheat or specialty flours, make sure you store it in the refrigerator or freezer or use it up quickly to avoid having it become rancid. Once you get used to making your baked goods from scratch using uncomplicated recipes, you will notice how much better and cheaper they are than packaged products. This is also a way to avoid the use of a lot of preservatives. Recently I purchased a fifty-pound bag of

52

unbleached flour for less than twenty cents per pound! I use it in my bread machine, too.

Sugar

I shop for white sugar where I get the best price, which I usually find to be at a shopping club in a ten-pound bag. Store in containers with a tight cover. I also buy brown and confectioners' sugar in two or four-pound bags and store in containers with tight covers. Sometimes you can find containers inexpensively or free, which is even better. Mine came from my place of work many years ago. Mayonnaise came in the gallon-sized jars with screw-on covers. I asked if I could have some if they were to be thrown away anyway. I'm sure they will last forever!

I plan on having the three types of sugars on hand all the time as basics: brown, white, and confectioners'. As I've said before if you have the basics on hand, you will be ready to make a variety of recipes. The three basic flavorings that I like to keep on hand are vanilla, maple, and almond. If my family liked mint flavoring, I would have kept that on hand also. I like the pure flavorings as opposed to the imitation; however, the imitation is much cheaper. Apparently now imitation flavorings and food colorings are safer than when I was raising my children. Buy what you can afford in the size that's the best price.

More About the Basics

I have a few more things to say about the basics. Try generics, if you don't notice a difference then continue to purchase them. I purchase the store brand powdered or canned milk for cooking. It is much cheaper to buy the powdered milk to use in baked products than fresh milk. The powdered milk keeps well in the cupboard in a tightly covered container. When I was on a tight budget I also made sweetened, condensed milk from instant skim milk powder. My recipe made the equivalent of two cans of sweetened, condensed milk that was also low in fat.

There are some basics that may seem like luxuries; however, I have found differently. I used to grease my pans with shortening, but then started using nonstick cooking sprays. I find that unless you overspray your pans, a can of spray lasts a long time. Store brand nonstick cooking sprays are now available, which is what I use. The sprays add less fat and are better for you than shortening to grease your baking pans. It is also a quicker and cleaner way to prepare your baking pans.

Several years ago I read that using a liquid lecithin is a good and cheap way to make your own cooking spray using a reusable spray container. Apparently you can even add olive or vegetable oil to the solution. I tried the lecithin but found it to be sticky and the bottle of lecithin was quite expensive at the health food store. It did work once you got it on the pan, which was awkward. I purchased the liquid lecithin for $2.79 for a sixteen-ounce bottle back in the 1980s. According to one source, lecithin is a good emulsifying agent, which causes a breakdown in cholesterol and fats in the blood. I'm not convinced that the small quantity that you would need to use each time would be that beneficial. Recently, I have tried using olive oil and a small amount of lecithin in a reusable spray bottle. I still can't seem to get a surface that is as nonstick as the commercially made nonstick cooking spray. I have also seen a recipe to prevent food from sticking to baking pans using a combination of 3 tablespoons flour, 3 tablespoons cornstarch, and ½ cup shortening, then mix together and brushed on pans. I have not tried this recipe.

Sea salt is the only kind of salt I have used for the past thirty years. I purchase this sea salt in the health food store very inexpensively and keep it in a jar in my cupboard. My understanding is that sea salt is better than regular table salt because it contains other beneficial seawater minerals. I recently bought some Maine sea salt while home on vacation. I guess because sea salt is now considered a gourmet item, it cost me about $5 for a fairly small amount. I don't notice the difference in taste except the Maine salt is coarser. It was definitely a frivolous, impulsive purchase that I never would have considered years ago. I reduce salt in many recipes, except when mixing up bread and pizza dough. For yeast products, you should use the exact amounts called for of yeast, sugar, and salt. The salt slows the yeast from rising and the sugar aids in the rising.

Most of the time it is cheaper to buy spices in a health food store in the amount you will use in a reasonable length of time. By using your own container for storage, the price will be lower since the health food store purchases in bulk. I also think the spices are fresher this way. We use a lot of dried oregano and I've found a store that carries good size bottles for less than a dollar, sometimes two for a dollar. I like to buy my cocoa in the health food store as well. The larger the bag you buy, the cheaper it is. I am able to buy Hershey's Dutch cocoa at a very good price. When the kids were young, I used to make my own cocoa mix for making hot cocoa. A large batch would carry us through the winter months, as it kept well in a tightly covered container.

Now living in southwestern Pennsylvania, I purchase my spices in bulk in either Mennonite or Amish stores. I no longer pour what I need from large containers but I still can purchase the size I need at a reasonable price in small plastic bags or tubs. I also buy cocoa, Jell-O, sanding sugar, dip mixes, pudding mixes, etc. in bulk packages.

Some of our favorite recipes call for dry onion soup mix. I find that making it from scratch in the amount I needed from dehydrated, chopped onion (that I buy in bulk) and powdered beef bouillon is a much cheaper alternative. With only two ingredients, it is also quick and simple to make!

Baking mix such as Bisquick, is a nice convenience, but was too expensive for my budget. I've found a comparable recipe to make a large batch. This is a quicker way to mix up pancakes or waffles than from scratch and cheaper than buying the popular brand baking mix. If you are a small family, the work involved to put the mix together might not be worth the time spent, especially if you don't use it within six months.

I think I have only bought maple-flavored pancake syrup once since I started having children. A friend shared with me that her family was always on a tight budget when she was growing up and they never had "store-bought" syrup. I make about a quart at a time, which keeps well in the refrigerator. The recipe is simple and quick to make. We like to heat it in the microwave before serving.

Yeast is much cheaper when purchased in the health food store, and it is a reputable brand. I buy about six ounces at a time and keep it in a pint-sized canning jar in my refrigerator. Yeast shouldn't be kept for a long period of time; it loses its potency. Buying it this way is much cheaper than buying the little packages. I use one heaping teaspoonful, equal to one package of yeast called for in recipes. Some shopping clubs and our local Mennonite stores carry brand name instant yeast in freeze-dried, one-pound packages at a very low price.

Croutons and breadcrumbs can be made easily and can be tastier than the packaged products. You don't have to use fresh bread for these. Store older bread in containers in the freezer if you aren't planning to use it up right away for croutons or bread crumbs. For breadcrumbs, dry the bread well in a slow oven; separate the slices on a baking sheet first. Once the bread is dry, place it in a food processor or blender to make fine crumbs, or you can place the dry bread in a plastic bag and crush with a rolling pin. Croutons can be made in the microwave or oven. You can make the croutons low fat if you want and experiment with flavors. See my favorite in the recipe section.

I used to buy cheese in five-pound blocks or bags and repackaged in meal size quantities. When I bought five-pound blocks of cheddar or chunks of Swiss cheese, I might have some sliced and leave the rest in a chunk and grate it myself. Grating is quick in a food processor, but I have had to do it before by using a hand grater. When I bought cheese in bulk, I had to freeze what I didn't want used right away or my family would snack on it until it was gone! When refrigerating cheese, wrap it well to prevent it from drying out.

I like to keep a package of pectin in my cupboard for making jams or jellies. Years ago I was planning on cooking pork roast for dinner. The recipe that I liked to use called for apple jelly in the sauce, but I discovered that I was out of it. The local store was three miles away and I'm not even sure I had a car available then. I had pectin in the cupboard and apple juice concentrate in the freezer so I was able to make the apple jelly that I needed. It was quick and easy to make. It's just nice to have the basics!

I can't say enough about safe food storage. There are a lot of good food storage guides available. Obtain one and post it inside your cupboard or outside of your large freezer. I use one that I found in a *Taste of Home* magazine.

Non-food Basics

I like to buy the best bar soap I can afford, take it out of the wrapper, and place in a large glass jar that I keep on a shelf in my bathroom for display. It adds a decorative touch and if you use different color soaps it looks nice. It might be the least expensive soap available, but it does look nice. I like liquid soap on the bathroom and kitchen sinks because it seems less messy to use and it is less work keeping the sink area clean and tidy. You can use the disposable soap dispensers and reuse or buy a decorative bathroom dispenser as you can afford. The decorative liquid soap dispensers would not have worked well when my kids were young because they are usually made out of a breakable material. The prefilled plastic dispensers were best during those years. One of these can be reused and refilled many times. I buy the liquid hand soap in gallon jugs at a shopping club at a very good price. Usually the gallon jug lasts nearly a year. When I first started using the cute little liquid soap containers, the kids would play with it, causing waste, but soon the novelty wore off and a little would go a long ways.

Experiment with laundry detergent. The more expensive brands certainly have the nicest scents. Many people think only a popular name brand detergent works best. I remember times when I could only afford the cheaper brands. I did not notice a big difference if any, except for the scent. Buy what you can afford. I have heard appliance repairmen say that you can use slightly less than the amount of detergent called for and still get good results and it will probably be better for your washing machine.

Body lotions vary a lot. I tend to buy the inexpensive brands that work well and place them in pretty reusable dispensers to display. Some lotions have nicer scents than others, but even the less pricey lotions are offered in different scents.

Cosmetics vary a lot in price. Remember that you don't have to buy the most expensive to find a good product. Don't waste lipsticks and cover-ups that come in tubes. When it seems like you are at the end of the tube, you still have up to a half inch left. I use a small instrument to remove the remainder. You can put it into a small reusable container or take it out a little at a time, as you need it. This is a big savings because make-up is expensive. I have also substituted lipstick for cream blush. This sometimes works best when blended with a little foundation.

You might not feel that you can afford to wear make-up; however, if you need a little color and it makes you feel better, I suggest you squeeze it into your budget. I see it as part of good grooming. And as one person once said, "If the barn needs painting, paint it!" My husband appreciates it!

Fabric softener sheets can be cut in half, using only a half for each dryer load. I have found that this works better when I use a better quality fabric softener sheet. I prefer to use liquid fabric softener. Carefully check prices. I have found that the largest size bottle of fabric softener in a shopping club isn't as inexpensive as a smaller size bottle of the same brand name fabric softener that I buy in Wal-Mart. The smaller container that I purchase is in a more concentrated form, thus allowing you to get more washer loads than the larger size. Check the labels carefully. Reducing slightly the amount of liquid fabric softener you use per load seems to work just as well.

There have been times, as I have mentioned before, that I have had to make drastic cuts in my shopping list in order to fit everything in. One way I did this was to use white vinegar in the place of fabric softener. I used ½ cup of white vinegar in the rinse cycle per laundry load. Vinegar removes the soap residue from the clothes and the laundry comes out fluffier from the dryer and static free; apparently it helps to soften line-dried clothes also. I have read recently that using vinegar in each laundry load might not be good for your machine. Using occasionally, I'm sure would be okay. I have not had a problem. Buy white vinegar in a gallon jug for increased savings. I buy the store brand with good results. There are many economical uses for white vinegar in both cooking and cleaning.

The bathroom cleaner that I purchase in pump spray form is a product that I have always tried to keep on hand. I am particular about the brand; I prefer Comet bathroom cleaner. It dissolves soap scum well and disinfects without a strong odor. I find bathroom cleaners vary a lot in how well they work. There are many new ones on the market now that weren't available years ago. The rule in our house was that if you were the last one in the shower you were to spray the shower and bathtub after finishing, then wipe down. This saves a lot of time and avoids having to scrub soap scum off later. It only takes a quick spray of the sink and toilet seat to make that cleanup quick and easy also. Obviously this isn't a job for young children.

When I was shopping monthly I knew exactly how many paper products we used per month and would replenish the stock. I find toilet paper varies a lot in quality and amount on a roll. The thickest is pricey and more apt to cause septic system problems. I think paper towels are overused and also vary in quality. I use only about one roll per month. Newspapers or a squeegee are great for washing windows and I use rags made from old T-shirts, cloth diapers, or towels for clean ups. In recent years I have purchased a large package of microfiber cloths just for cleaning. They work very well for washing windows and mirrors. The cloths wash well and dry quickly.

I need to say more about using vinegar since it is such a versatile product. Besides cooking and using as a fabric softener, it can be used as a stain remover; it removes mineral deposits from coffeepots, ice cube trays, and water pitchers. Vinegar can make copper pans shiny again by mixing ½ tablespoon of salt with ½ cup vinegar. Use vinegar as a rinse after shampooing to remove soap build up from your hair. Use a small amount of vinegar in a cup of water in your microwave on high until boiling. Let sit for a few minutes then wipe the inside clean with a damp absorbent cloth. This cleans as well as deodorizes. Distilled white vinegar can also be used in a diluted solution as a window wash or to deodorize cloth diapers or towels. My daughter always uses white vinegar when washing her son's cloth diapers. She also uses a white vinegar water solution to spray on her shower to remove soap scum. She says that after spraying the tub she wipes it with a microfiber cloth to remove the soap scum. She is concerned about using safer products in her home around young children. My generation didn't seem to think about being environmentally safe, but it is a good idea. One source I was reading listed forty-six uses of vinegar, most of which were not for cooking purposes. Do your research if you are interested in safe, inexpensive products.

Baking soda is another inexpensive product that isn't just for cooking. It's great to use as a non-abrasive cleaner for surface stains on counters and on flooring. It's a good deodorizer also. Read the many uses listed on the container.

Ammonia is a cleaning product that is both inexpensive and versatile; however, never mix it with bleach. A bleach and ammonia mixture can produce a potentially fatal inhalant. Always use ammonia solutions in a well-ventilated area. I purchase the plain ammonia without soap. For most of my married life I have used an ammonia and water solution as a window cleaner. I use a reusable spray container and about ½ cup of ammonia with about twelve to sixteen ounces of water. There are other recipes using ammonia as a window cleaner. Another one that I have used that works well is two ounces household ammonia, four ounces rubbing alcohol, and ½ teaspoon dish detergent (I like Dawn), in about sixteen ounces of water. This recipe is good because it keeps windows frost-free. Another window cleaner recipe that works well is one quart water, ½ cup ammonia, and ⅓ cup white vinegar. This will cut grease and dirt and leave the glass streak free.

Ammonia is a good wax remover on floors; however, if you have no-wax flooring read the manufacturer's instructions first. Ammonia also can be used to remove soap scum from shower doors. Using a plastic mesh scrubber in a 50/50 ammonia and water solution, lightly scrub the surface then let sit for a while, reapply as needed. Rinse with clean water and wipe dry with a soft dry cloth. Mom taught me to add a little ammonia to the soap and water when washing hair combs and brushes to remove dirt and hairspray build up effectively.

Bleach is also a good cleaning and disinfecting product to have on hand. I buy the gallon size, which is more economical. You have to decide if the store brand is as good as a name brand. I have not seen a significant difference. Pouring undiluted bleach directly on fabrics can cause holes. Not only does bleach whiten white cotton fabrics when used in a dilute solution, it can also disinfect cutting boards and countertops. While living in Central America we had to wash our fruits and vegetables in a weak bleach solution before eating. When a friend told me to soak my lettuce in bleach and water solution I thought I could never stand to eat it afterward. However, by using 1 tablespoon of household bleach to 1 gallon of water and allowing the lettuce to soak for twenty minutes, then placing in a clean pillowcase, spinning out the water in my washer at the end of the final spin cycle, the lettuce was safe to eat and did not have a bleach taste, since the water was spun out well. Another use for bleach is to add about 1 teaspoon bleach and 1 teaspoon sugar to a pint of water in a vase. This helps to keep flowers fresh longer.

Cent-sible Health Care

Over-the-counter medications can be very expensive. My suggestion is to buy generic or store brands and use appropriately. Keep all medications out of the reach of children, including over the counter medications and prescription medications. Don't let children dispense their own meds. You might think your nine and ten-year-olds are mature enough but parents are responsible for giving their children medication.

For headaches, general body aches, or to reduce a fever that is over 101 degrees give acetaminophen. Don't use more than the recommended dosage or use more often than recommended. A medication such as acetaminophen seems very safe, but can be fatal if taken in large amounts. My understanding is that if you have a cold or flu, a low grade temp up to 100 degrees for a couple of days is therapeutic for healing. If it's over 101 degrees you medicate or become concerned. If it's a baby under one year old, always notify the physician. Never give any over the counter meds to a child under one year old without the advice of the baby's physician.

For muscle aches, menstrual cramps, or as a fever reducer, if acetaminophen is not effective, take ibuprofen as directed on the product literature. Naproxen sodium is effective for muscle aches, menstrual cramps, or as a fever reducer also.

Both ibuprofen and naproxen sodium should be taken with food because they can cause stomach upset. Ibuprofen seems to work well as an anti-inflammatory medication in higher dosages that your physician could recommend.

For colds or flu, I did not give my family the multisymptom, over-the-counter meds because usually they were expensive and we didn't have all the symptoms that the medication treated. Treat the symptoms that you have. If your nose is stuffy or you have post nasal drip, use a decongestant such as pseudoephedrine.

If you need an antihistamine for allergy symptoms, take Benadryl. An antihistamine can be used for bee stings, itchy poison ivy, allergic reactions, or hives to name a few. Benadryl 25mg capsules are sold over the counter. Benadryl should only be taken every six hours and because it can cause drowsiness, you should not drive or operate machinery while taking it. Do not increase the dose unless you consult your physician first. If it is not effective or your condition worsens, you should consult your physician.

Talk with your physician before you need to take over-the-counter medications and ask what he suggests that you and your family take and have those medications available.

For infants and children, always check with their physician. Usually babies and children are given acetaminophen, ibuprofen, or naproxen sodium according to their weight, not their age. This might have changed so check with your doctor. An infant eight weeks old or under with a fever of 100.5 degrees or greater should always be seen by the doctor. Don't give cold medications to babies under one year of age or to any child without first speaking with your physician. Also, take your child's temperature if he/she is sick, since the more information you have to tell the doctor, the better prepared he will be to diagnose the problem. Some things to notice when assessing your child's condition are: temperature, breathing difficulty, cough (productive or dry), sore throat, color (pale or flushed), and location of pain. Is your child rubbing his/her ears? Is your child listless? Does he/she have a dry mouth. How many wet diapers has he/she had in the past eight to twenty-four hours, is the urine stronger than usual, is there a change in stools (watery, mucousy, bloody)? Is he/she aroused easily or confused? How long has he/she been sick? When given acetaminophen, ibuprofen, or naproxen sodium did his/her temperature come down below 101 degrees within an hour?

Prescription medication and general first-aid information is important to know as well. If you are taking prescription medications, always check with your doctor before taking any over-the-counter meds along with your prescription medications. Watch for expiration dates. Store all medications appropriately out of reach of children. Always finish your prescription, even if you feel better, unless your physician tells you differently. This is especially important when taking antibiotics. Watch for and report side effects when on a new medication.

I keep a triple antibiotic ointment on hand for cuts and abrasions; after cleansing the area with mild soap and water, apply only a thin coat as necessary. Cover the wound with a band aid or dressing as needed to contain bleeding and keep clean and dry.

Hydrocortisone cream 1% usually relieves itchy rashes or sunburn discomfort. Using cool compresses topically, taking acetaminophen, and avoiding new contact with the sun can be helpful in treating sunburn discomfort, unless it's severe. For treating first-degree burns, those with only redness, treat with cold water. Cover any blisters to protect from breaking, which could lead to an infection. I have found that covered first-degree burns feel more comfortable than those left open to the air. Watch and report any increased redness and signs of infection.

Lotrimin 1% cream is a good over the counter anti-fungal cream. Use a thin coat twice a day until clear. It's often used to treat external yeast infections.

Be prepared for emergencies. To make a reusable warm compress, take two 12" x 5" pieces of cotton fabric (use natural fabrics since some synthetic fabrics could melt in the microwave) and sew three of the sides together. Fill loosely with approximately 1 ½ cups of uncooked rice (not minute rice) then sew the end closed. It's best to use fabric that's not too thin and has a tight weave. This bag can be microwaved on high for one minute or less, depending on your microwave. Check to make sure it's not so hot that it will cause a burn. Apply the heated bag for only twenty minutes at a time three to four times daily to the affected part. The warm bag works well, since it conforms to the body part and stays warm for at least twenty minutes. Although I like to use the rice because I always have it on hand, buckwheat hulls also work well.

To make a reusable ice pack, fill a pint or quart-sized zip type freezer bag with ¾ cup water and ¼ cup rubbing alcohol. You might want to double bag this to reduce the chance of leaking. Try to get all of the air out of the bag so it will conform to the body part better. Label the bag well and store the filled bag in the freezer until needed. To use, wrap the bag with a lightweight cloth or place in a pillowcase and apply for no more than twenty minutes at a time. To help it stay on an extremity, try wrapping loosely with an ace bandage. In a pinch you can use a bag of frozen vegetables for a quick ice pack.

If you want to try these suggestions, remember to ask

your doctor if he agrees with the treatments. Use prescription medications as your doctor prescribes. Watch for side effects or adverse reactions and report to your doctor as necessary. Finish all prescription medications as prescribed. Think safety in your home and as a mom; observe symptoms of illness in your family carefully. If you have questions or concerns, call your doctor's office with all of the symptoms. Sometimes it won't require a doctor's visit. I use generic, over the counter medications. If you are not sure what the generic name is, ask a pharmacist.

Learn how to take your child's temperature. Keep a thermometer for children and adults on hand. The more information you can give your doctor about your child's illness, the easier it will be for him to treat your child. Encourage good and frequent hand washing and practice it yourself. This can make a big difference in passing germs from one person to the next.

Make sure you take your child for the recommended immunizations at the appropriate age. We can be so thankful for the availability of immunizations. It was so sad to see children in Honduras, Central America dying of tetanus due to the parents' unawareness of how to get immunization services that were available.

Home Organization, Maintenance, and Learning

I have already talked about kitchen organization and basic maintenance; however, to add a little more regarding the rest of the house is important. It really doesn't matter whether you own your home or rent, you need to be responsible for how you take care of it. We own a home in Maine; however, we rent a farmhouse in Pennsylvania. When we moved here there was a lot of work to be done, as I talk about more in a later chapter. I don't treat my living space any differently in a rental home than I do in my own. Unless I'm away, ill, or have guests, I'm pretty consistent with regular housework. I make my bed every day and taught my children to do the same. I also dust and vacuum weekly, clean the bathrooms daily as needed, keep mirrors clean, remove clutter, and straighten up the house before I go to bed. I don't spend a lot of time cleaning because I do a little regularly to prevent big clean ups. In the morning before I leave the bedroom, I make the bed and pick up. Clothes go in the hamper when they are dirty. After I'm finished getting ready for the day I make sure the bathroom is clean and picked up. I keep bathroom spray cleaner in each bathroom, as well as a toilet brush. Having the cleaning tools at hand where they will be used makes it easy to do quick clean ups. When I run out of a cleaning product, I either make up more such as window cleaner or put the item on the grocery list. Line your wastebaskets with the plastic bags you get your groceries in. Empty wastebaskets every evening when you take out the garbage. I taught the kids to pick up their toys and had a place for them to put them. Even if you have only a cardboard box for toys, it will keep the child's room or play area looking neater. I don't like to have to clean around a lot of clutter so it's easier to take care of it.

What husband doesn't like to come home to relax in an organized home? Usually the husband will follow your example if you are consistent. You are a team and marriage is about respect for each other. Steve knows I like the house neat and I know he doesn't like to come home to chaos. This might sound a little old-fashioned but I like to have the house in order and look well groomed when Steve comes home from work. I felt this way even when I was raising three children and working three days a week. I know he always appreciated it. In turn, he has always helped me as he saw the need.

In the home, the husband-wife relationship lasts a whole lot longer than the mother-child relationship in the home. Children grow up and leave much too quickly. It's a wise choice to make time for enjoying your spouse while raising children; make it a priority. I also want to stress enjoying your children as much as possible. It's a wonderful stage in all of your lives and it prepares you to enjoy them in a whole different way as they become adults. Don't take your spouse and children for granted. Thank the Lord every day for how you have been blessed. Try to be positive; it is contagious!

Sometimes it has been easier for me to rush through my routine of home organization and maintenance without taking time to teach the children or asking them to help. This is an area that I wish I would have spent more time in. My kids were involved in sports, Boy Scouts, and church activities so I didn't push them. I should have taught them more about laundry, ironing, and basic sewing and given them more responsibility in those areas. My first concern was their responsibility to their homework and the activities that they committed to participate in. They did have dinner time responsibilities, feeding pets, taking out the trash, sweeping the garage, putting away their clean clothes, and making their beds, but doing laundry, ironing, and mending weren't chores I gave them. I tried to give a crash course before they went away to college, but that was too late. Sarah always insisted that she would hire a maid when she was an adult so she wouldn't need that information! There were many times I wished there was a book on how to raise children and run a household on a budget. I suppose there was, but I would have been too busy to read it. It should have been required reading in order to get a marriage license! Mentoring is so important for young married couples. I think in my generation pride got in the way and we thought we knew it all or should know it all so we didn't ask. I wish someone had told me to lighten up and enjoy my relationships more. We did like to laugh a lot though, and humor in the home is a wonderful thing.

Besides the routine of daily upkeep of the home, windows do need to be washed periodically, as well as floors, walls, etc. Set up an easy plan. Try one area a month if you don't like to spring clean. Sometimes I would take a week off from work and spring or fall clean, but if that doesn't work for you, clean a small area a little at a time. Again, it is so easy to keep the house clean if you don't have a lot of stuff and keep the clutter down.

Years ago it was a given that you changed your sheets weekly, but I see a lot of people not doing that. Have you ever heard of dust mites? People get allergic reactions to dust mites and that's another reason to dust, vacuum, wash curtains, and change sheets. After washing and drying clothes, don't leave them in the dryer or in a clothesbasket, but fold or hang them up. If you don't, it's so easy to become overwhelmed and not do it because there is so much to do. The clothes become wrinkled and need ironing and then you have so many to put away. It's exhausting for me to just think about. It's so much easier to just do it. You can combine it with watching the news, talking on the phone, getting dinner.

Organize your bedrooms comfortably. Besides the obvious bed and place to store clothes, try to provide a chair, reading lamp, a place to store toys and books, and a wastebasket. A nightstand or shelf beside the bed, warm blankets, and comfortable pillows are essential and don't have to be expensive. For your children, provide a bulletin board to hang mementos on. If they share a bedroom, try to give each child his own space within the room. Treat what you have with respect and care and teach that to your children. Teach them to respect others' property also. If you are raising children, ask yourself, How do I want my children to act and be received as adults? Then raise them that way. If your children see disrespect, rudeness, sloppiness, selfishness, uncleanliness, jealousy, dishonesty, and gossiping in you, chances are they will have many of the same traits as adults. I'm not saying I didn't battle any of those traits, but I knew that I wanted my children to be good, caring, respectful adults and my husband and I had to work to be good examples. Whether you are a Christian or not, I feel that this is essential.

One thing I have learned from my life about home organization and maintenance is that the more stuff you accumulate, the more difficult it is to keep organized and take care of what you have. When we lived in Honduras, where people lived simply and life was slow, it was a shock to return home and find people so busy working to buy, use, and maintain stuff. Living like this leaves little time for your family and friends. I can be just as guilty if I don't occasionally reflect on how I live.

Hospitality

There have been a lot of books written on hospitality by Christian women. I have read many of them because this is an area that I feel the Lord has called me. I am interested in this area, but I struggle in it also. The real me would like everything to be perfect: the house with a guestroom, the food, the kids. Well, that isn't reality, and the perfectionist part of me continues to struggle. We have a modest home, no guestroom, normal kids, and a conservative budget. It would be easy to avoid inviting people into our home for meals or to spend the night. Now the kids are grown and most of the time only my husband and I are here at home. We did invite people in for meals or fellowship during those early child rearing years and I'm so glad that we did. If I kept our home basically neat and clean, entertaining at the last minute was fairly easy. I encourage you to open your home to others for Bible studies, birthday parties, holiday parties, etc. We have had many teen youth group meetings and parties at our home over the years. We didn't have perfect furniture. Most pieces were old hand-me-downs or refinished pieces. I made new slipcovers, cushions, or pillows as needed. Taking good care of what you have by keeping it clean and in good repair is all that is needed. Arrange your furniture in a way that makes your visitor feel comfortable and enables you to talk together.

In our modest Maine home, our kitchen, dining, and living room spaces are open to one another. This enables us to have more people together, but prevents privacy, which works okay. We don't have a guestroom in our home. We only had three bedrooms for five people. If we had overnight visitors, we would make do with what we had. At times we have given up our bedroom and master bath to visiting missionaries to ensure their comfort and privacy. It was well worth the inconvenience, though, as their visits were such a blessing and cultural education for our family.

Treat your guests well, pamper them, and make sure they have plenty of towels, an extra blanket, and closet space. Try to anticipate their needs. I remember one year we were having a missionary couple stay at our home for two nights. I hadn't ever entertained an overnight guest that we didn't know or were not related to. It was our oldest son, Chris', first year of college and we were really short of cash that month; we didn't have decent towels or washcloths. I went shopping with what little I had for food and extras. I bought a couple of towels on sale and found a package of dishcloths on the clearance shelf that were striped and looked more like washcloths. I took them home and laundered them. Placing a small basket on my bathroom counter, I rolled up the "washcloths" and placed them in the basket by the bathroom sink. I hung the two new towels on the rack, made sure the bed linens were clean and neat, and plenty of closet space was available. I placed another little basket on my bureau and filled it with some small items such as lotion, chapstick, a disposable razor, a small tube of toothpaste (a sample given to me at the dentist's office), cough drops, mints, some chocolate, tissues, antacids, and a nice welcome note.

We were away at a teen youth group activity when they arrived. Our pastor let them into the house. I had made corn chowder for their supper and some ham and cheese sandwiches in small sub rolls. I left notes about the food and where their room was located. This worked out well because they had a chance to eat, get settled in, and rested before our family overwhelmed them. They were such a blessing to have in our home. Our kids enjoyed their African adventure stories and learned firsthand about a new culture, as well as how the Lord had worked in their life. Food was simple, but hearty. Often guests are overfed, so remember each meal doesn't have to be a feast. Ask ahead about their food or dietary preferences. When they leave, write on an index card little things about them, such as their likes and dislikes, and note the things you might do differently if they come again. It might be several years before they are back in the States on a visit, and with my short memory I would forget the little, important details.

In Honduras, the Lord challenged me. I was not working for the first time in my life and only had one child moving with us and she was seventeen years old. We were blessed to have a large house with five bathrooms. As soon as we got moved in and purchased furniture and household items, we contacted some local missionaries I had learned about prior to moving by contacting various mission boards in the United States. I went to Honduras with a list of names and phone numbers. We felt led to open our home to traveling missionaries that would come into the city on business or to be near the airport after coming in or before leaving the country. We met many neat people this way and learned a lot about hospitality. It wasn't unusual to have someone staying in our home that we had never met before.

We were able to buy nice, new furniture at that time. Since

we had no small children, we were not as careful with choosing light-colored fabrics for the furniture. Our dining room table was large, made of black lacquered wood with a glass top. The chairs were shiny black lacquered wood with white fabric seats. Very elegant looking in our new dining room! This was great for nearly "empty nesters" like us, or so we thought. The Lord was to do a work in us! Everything was new in this house, including new sheets and towels, and new comforters on all the beds. One of the first missionary families we hosted had two young children, six years and two years old. Well, guess what happened when the two-year-old ate her spaghetti at the table? You're right, red spaghetti sauce was all over that chair! Our first reaction was to get upset (without showing it, of course). We could have easily been overprotective of all of our new things and stopped inviting people in, but the Lord knew our weak areas and I think we were put to a test. Because of our commitment to hospitality, we had to let go of the shiny, clean chairs with the white seats and anything else that we were blessed with. What an education and blessing we received from these dear friends and the spaghetti sauce didn't even stain the chair! What a good God we serve!

If you can't afford to invite people in for a meal, make it a potluck meal with everyone contributing. I use my company meal index cards for meal and dessert ideas. Because I used the same plan in Honduras regarding food staples, I could take my recipe box and come up with a meal idea using what I had. One meal might be roasting two small chickens (the only size chickens available were small), and saving leftovers for the next night's sweet and sour chicken over rice. I like to pamper guests, as I would like to be pampered. For many years we couldn't afford to go out to dinner so when I am the hostess, I like to treat my guests as if they were at a fine restaurant. I like to have plenty of the food I can afford to serve, glassware that matches, cloth napkins, and maybe candles. Just a nice relaxing atmosphere! If you feel that you can't invite guests for even a potluck meal, invite them in for dessert and coffee.

For large parties such as birthdays or graduations, I set up my kitchen bar as a serve-yourself buffet. You can place the drinks on another counter top. Sometimes we serve hot dogs from the grill, "make your own" sub sandwiches, or maybe homemade pizza. The memories are worth the effort. If you prepare early in the day and wash the dishes as you go, cleanup will be quick and easy. Try to get the whole family involved.

On Christmas Eve I like having friends and family come to our home. I serve simple foods and drinks. This has become a special tradition. A few years ago I decided to purchase an inexpensive red three-ring notebook on which I wrote *Christmas Book* using a black marker. In it I include information for the holidays, such as a list of the names of those I buy gifts for and another page that lists the names of those I send Christmas cards to. On this page I also include the year, and a box to check off recording who I received cards from. An address section is quick reference when addressing Christmas cards. Now I have a copy of my address list that I use in my computer to print my address labels. Also, I put in a copy of each year's Christmas letter that I send out. My notebook includes the Christmas Eve menu that I served and the accompanying recipes. In this notebook I placed Christmas dinner contributions to take to my mother's, including the amounts and recipes. I put pictures in my notebook of how I decorated our home during the holidays. The pictures of my Christmas decorating certainly helped when it came time to decorate each year. This notebook probably saved me more time each year than it took to prepare it. I wished I had made one many years ago.

Webster's dictionary describes hospitality as "entertaining guests in a friendly, generous manner." [1] In the New Testament, Paul tells us to be "given to hospitality" (Romans 12:13, NIV). I just can't say enough about hospitality. We have received such blessings from it and made great memories. The more often you invite people in the easier it gets. Don't wait until you have a perfect house with perfect furniture and lots of money to serve perfect meals, because then you will be hesitant to get your perfect stuff soiled, as we found out while in Honduras. Share what the Lord has blessed you with. Your guests will never know you were short of cash or material items if you treat them with graciousness and are confident while using what you have. Simple is a good thing with the right heart!

My New Adventure in Homemaking as an "Empty Nester"

In my wildest dreams I never believed that in our fifties we would have to move from our comfortable life in Maine, where our family and friends are, to a rural Amish neighborhood in southwestern Pennsylvania. I know other people have job losses and have to move, but I just didn't really expect it would be us. It's not that I didn't see the closing of my husband's company coming, it is that I just expected the Lord to provide another position close to home. Well, we did have to move, we took a big pay cut, I had to leave my part-time job and more importantly our family, and we had to do it sooner than I had expected. "I don't understand this, Lord, this is where our family and ministry are," I complained. When you say, "Take my life, Lord, and use me," you need to be ready to be used. We needed to make the most of our situation and not complain about it if it couldn't be changed. Would I want to be where I wanted to be, or be in the Lord's will and where He wanted me to be? We chose what we believed to be the Lord's will for us. We rented out our Maine home and moved to southwestern Pennsylvania.

Since the move, we have many stories of how the Lord worked in our lives at just the moment that we needed him. The first house we rented was for sale, but in the months we lived there it had not been shown until we decided to rent an old farmhouse on a picturesque country road. The day that Steve was to call our landlord to tell him we would be moving, our landlord called us and said that he had someone interested in buying the house. This was our affirmation from the Lord that we were making the right move. The farmhouse had been home to a wonderful Mennonite family, the Mausts, for many, many years. They had raised seven children there and had hosted Fresh Air Kids for many years. I'm sure they were not financially well off; he was a farmer and carpenter and she, a homemaker. They were a wonderful Christian family whose hospitality was well known in the area. We have heard wonderful stories of their hospitality from their former Fresh Air Kids and many local families.

My Amish friend Rhoda feels the Lord wanted Steve and me here to carry on the Maust family tradition in hospitality. I didn't realize what the Maust family was like until after I had redecorated and was considering opening a small bed and breakfast because of our beautiful surroundings, having plenty of room, and my interest in hospitality. Rhoda didn't know anything about us when she and her husband, Henry, decided to rent to us, but sensed it was the right thing to do. The Lord has blessed us with reasonable rent and plenty of space in this comfortable home. Steve and some good friends of ours doubted my sanity when we first looked at the house, but they really love it now. We have had the opportunity to completely redecorate, which involved seven months of constant hard work in order to make it comfortable and attractive on a budget. We will be able to return it to Henry and Rhoda in better condition when we one day return to Maine, to our own house. To make a long story short, the farmhouse is next door to a wonderful Bible-believing church where we are now active, our Amish neighbors are a delight, and, although we do not have a bed and breakfast, we are able to open our home as a ministry as the need arises. I'm a full-time homemaker much to my delight and I'm able to use my skills to benefit others. I still shop carefully, cook quite a lot, but give away a significant amount. I have learned a lot about thrift and cooking from Rhoda and her daughters and their Amish ways. Also, our pastor and his wife have twelve children. They are such a good testimony in thrift, hospitality, homemaking, and godly child rearing.

Moving here has been an education that I know God would have me share with others. One thing I have learned is that you can't out-give God. We receive so much from others, especially our Amish friends. I have received steak; pork chops; sausage; a ten-pound, free range, hand-plucked chicken; hamburger; cakes; cookies; homemade donuts and pies. When I have had to go home to Maine for extended periods, our Amish friends and others have taken good care of Steve.

When we first moved to this area I thought that it was so far from a Wal-Mart, wholesale club, and other large stores. Usually I think of the larger stores as places where you can get some of the best bargains. I had always bought my flour, cocoa, and spices in a health food store, but I could not find one near here. I did not realize at the time that there are a lot of small Amish and Mennonite-run stores in the country-side around here. They usually carry bulk foods, flour, sugar, spices, cheeses, jams, jellies, pie fillings, etc. In fact, my land-lords, Henry and Rhoda, own one of these stores, which carries much more than I have listed, including Henry's maple syrup. I can buy most of what I need for cooking right in my rural area at a very good price. Besides Rhoda's store, there is an Amish-run seasonal fruit and vegetable stand that also sells fresh eggs year round and Amish-made scatter rugs. Rhoda and Henry take orders for fresh fruit and vegetables in bulk during the fruit and vegetable season. The peaches, apples, grapes, etc. are so fresh and good and at a great price.

Most of the people living in this area of Pennsylvania aren't very prosperous. Many people burn wood or coal for heat and live a frugal lifestyle. There are several stores in this area that sell liquidation type food products such as dented cans, closeout products, products close to their expiration date, broken case lots, etc. These are great places to find bargains. I have not had a problem yet with the quality of the products. I'm careful to check dates and I examine the containers for leaks, bulging lids, or obvious signs of spoilage. I don't buy cans that are dented in a seam or are grossly dented. The stores I shop would refund a bad product. I have discussed how cooking from scratch can be economical and living in this area verifies that. I can have pantry basics on hand as well as do bulk shopping for the freezer and be ready for company, or to provide an unexpected meal that someone is in need of.

It's not unusual for us to have a fair amount of overnight company. If we were living in Maine right now, we probably would not have nearly the quality time with our family and friends as we enjoy when they come and stay with us for a week or two. Just before my mother became ill with leukemia, she, my sister, and my niece came for a visit that was so much fun. We had several days to just enjoy each other.

What memories I have of those last healthy days that my mother would know. What a blessing!

One thing I have learned from the Amish is simple living, although sometimes their lives are anything but simple. We tend to be a disposable society. When something breaks, we replace it. The Amish repair what they can. They grow much of what they eat and preserve the surplus. They even can their meat and poultry. Some freeze their produce, meats, and poultry. They are usually very organized, doing laundry on certain days and baking on certain days. They always set aside Sunday as a day of worship. If they have large household tasks, they have family and friends in to help. They always help others as needed. Reading is a great pastime that they enjoy, as well as visiting.

One day, two Amish children (whose parents are friends of ours), stopped in after school at my invitation to have cookies and cider for a snack. We had the most delightful conversation. We were talking about them going home and having to do their chores when Sharon, who is seven years old, said to me, "What do you do all day anyway?" I had to stop and think, *What do I do all day?* I tried to tell her and compared to their list of duties, I guess right now I don't have a long list of things I have to do. If I worked outside of the home now I wouldn't have the flexibility to travel with my husband on business or go home to see the family when Steve has long weekends or vacations. I volunteer at the local nursing home once a week, spending time visiting many of the residents. Once a month, I go on a bus ride with several of them and help them shop. As an "empty nester" there are so many ways to help others, especially if you are not working outside of the home. I have time to sew curtains for family or friends. I volunteer with Helping Hands at our church. I attend a weekly woman's Bible study and am available to take

Amish friends to appointments as needed. Last year before Easter, instead of buying my granddaughters an Easter basket filled with goodies, I bought two baskets that looked like old-fashioned picnic baskets. I bought some fabric with two different-colored children's prints and lined the baskets. I also made a small picnic tablecloth, napkin, and bag to hold a plate, cup, etc. for each granddaughter. I bought inexpensive, colorful plastic plates, bowls, drinking cups, and eating utensils for each one. I filled the baskets with goodies I had picked up, but kept the picnic gear separate until after they opened the basket. The idea was that they would bring the baskets to our house in the summertime and we would go on a picnic, which we did. We went to a beautiful (free) picnic area in the mountains of West Virginia and had great fun.

I said that our house took seven months to set up as a comfortable home. I also said that we have opened it up to being used as a hospitality home. We have set aside the whole upstairs living area for guests. It has three bedrooms, a sitting room, and a full bath. We have tried to pay attention to detail, often using old furniture that we have painted and repaired as needed. Some of our furniture is our landlord's, some given to us, and some antique. We made sure that we had a bed, dresser, chair, nightstand, reading light, clock, fan (we don't have air conditioning), and towel holder in each room. It's important to have plenty of blankets and pillows also. The sitting room has a loveseat that folds out into a twin bed, chair, a wicker chest used as a coffee table, a desk, and chair; a small refrigerator; a TV; VCR; and a DVD player. We do not have large rooms. In the bathroom I keep extra razors, shampoo, lotion, toothbrushes, soap, little sewing kits, etc., as well as a blow dryer and curling iron. We don't have any closets upstairs. Since this is an old house Steve put together a board with wrought iron hooks on one wall of each room to hold coat hangers; this is the closet! Also, we put a hook on the back of each door. The rooms are simply decorated, neat, and clean. I think this works well. When you look out of the windows and see horses and buggies, then "simple" works! The rooms are delightfully old-fashioned and I continuously receive complements on them. Often people visiting have heard about my redecorating and request to see the whole house. I love floral fabrics, color, and a cottage decorating style.

We are now in a new phase of ministry. About three months ago we were asked to take in two seventeen-year-old girls, not related to one another but in need of a place to live so they could each finish their senior year of high school in our town. Their single mothers would be moving to different states. The day after we returned home from our Christmas vacation in Maine, the girls came to live with us. What a blessing they were; I can't say it was always easy on all of us getting to know each other and living together, but it went very well. I can honestly say that from the beginning I never had a moment's doubt about whether or not we did the right thing. I believe that if the Lord gives you a ministry, He will equip you for it, and He graciously has. You just need to be willing to be used and if it is from the Lord, you will have peace. Now I have been given a new challenge in *Cent-sible Homemaking*!

Naomi, Pastor's Wife, Mother of 12 Children

The Lord has given me the wonderful opportunity of meeting a very special woman who has been a tremendous blessing to me. The lessons to be learned from Naomi are things I just have to share with you. Besides being a godly pastor's wife, mother to twelve children, grandmother to one, Bible study and Sunday school teacher, she has and is homeschooling all of her children, sings with her husband and children professionally, frequently takes meals and visits those in need, and on and on and on. I have never met anyone like her. By the way, did I mention that her home is very neat and clean also? This can be attributed to the fact that she is consistent and organized. She also loves to pray and makes her Lord Jesus her first love in her life and it shows.

I asked her if she would be willing to let me share with others some of her thoughts and the ways that she accomplishes *Cent-sible Homemaking* in her busy life. I gave her a list of questions and she shared with me some of her thoughts and approaches.

First of all, since this book is mainly about how to feed

your family economically, I asked her what her favorite economical family recipe is. This is the recipe that she gave me:

1-2-3-4 Casserole

2 pounds hamburger with chopped onions (both uncooked), salt and pepper
1 quart green beans, drained
enough raw peeled, sliced potatoes to cover the top of the layers
In a greased 9"x13" baking pan, place hamburger with chopped onions, salt, and pepper on the bottom. Next, layer the drained green beans. The next layer is enough peeled, sliced potato to cover the top of the layers. Then mix in a bowl:
2 cans cream of mushroom soup with 3 cups milk or water

Pour this mixture over the layers and bake, covered at 350 degrees for 1½ hours.

I next asked Naomi what she found to be helpful (besides the obvious "lots of money") in feeding her large family well and economically. She said that shopping at discount stores in our area such as Aldi, Dollar General, and Save-a-Lot are helpful in saving money. She doesn't use brand name products, she constantly checks for the best prices, and she keeps their meals "simple but nutritious and interesting." They use the less expensive foods such as potatoes, rice, pasta, hamburger, chicken, and venison.

Naomi also told me some of the ways she maintains her home efficiently on a budget. She buys according to needs rather than wants. For clothes, they shop at thrift stores, Wal-Mart, Value City, Dollar General, and similar types of stores that sell for less. They also have a lot of clothes given to them, which she has to be willing to go through to find what they can use, even though the items may not always be exactly what they want. She says they have chosen to be grateful and settle for what they have, "in balance." They don't buy anything on credit. She says, "If we don't have the money up front, then we take it as a don't-buy item, including vehicles." They borrowed money for their first house and that was with a low interest loan thru Joe's (her husband) dad.

I wanted to know how they fit hospitality into their busy lives and how they do that economically. Naomi stated, "We intentionally look for ways to open our home to welcome people needing friends, counsel, encouragement, and Jesus. We teach and believe the principle in Mark 9:37 about welcoming Jesus when we welcome children. Also, the principle of doing for the least of these we have done it for Jesus (paraphrased from Matthew 25:40). We love people because of the love that Jesus gives us. So Joe and I have tried to be examples of that to our children. They know our home is open to love people in whatever way we can. It's been so exciting to see our children care for people in the same way." Then she says, "When it comes to serving food, I use the guidelines: make what you can with what you have. So my food menu is what I can make with what I already have on hand and of course, I pray and ask the Lord to help me make something good, tasty, yet without spending lots of money. I've been blessed over and over as I feel the Lord giving the ideas on how to make good-tasting food or refreshments with what I already have. Along with that, I try to plan ahead and have food on hand for unexpected company." Hearing this from Naomi validates my feelings on replenishing the staples in the pantry and freezer as you can afford.

Recipes

Assuming that many of my readers are new to cooking, I have tried to clarify most of the recipe instructions. I have some recipes that were given to me that I don't feel I should change because it was an old family or friend's words or instructions. Please read through the entire recipe before making. Some of the ingredients might be within the recipe and not in the ingredients list. Also, some of my recipes are very old, handed-down recipes that didn't have cooking temperatures or times because of using a wood stove.

Appetizers, Pickles, and Relish

This is an easy way to make hardboiled eggs when you need a dozen at a time.

Hard-Boiled Eggs

Place the uncooked eggs into a large pan and add cold water to about one inch above the top of the eggs. Bring to a boil, remove from the heat when they come to a boil, cover and don't uncover for twenty minutes. Drain, then cover with cold water. The eggs should be just right!

Deviled Eggs

12 hard-cooked eggs
1 teaspoon salt
1 teaspoon dried mustard
¼ teaspoon black pepper
6 tablespoons salad dressing or mayonnaise

Cut peeled eggs lengthwise in half. Slip out yolks, mash with fork. Mix in seasonings and salad dressing. Fill whites with egg yolk mixture, heaping it up lightly. Using a pastry bag with a star tip makes the eggs look especially nice. Sprinkle with a little paprika for color.

My long-time friend, Jane, put the following recipe in one of our local cookbooks a long time ago. It makes a quick lunch on English muffins or a nice appetizer when spread on small slices of party rye bread. When my sister-in-law's kids were little and playing on summer baseball leagues, she would make these in the food booth to sell; she said they were a big hit.

Mini Pizzas

1-6-ounce can tomato paste
½ cup margarine, softened
1-12-ounce block sharp cheese, shredded
2 teaspoons dried oregano
1 teaspoon garlic salt

Mix well. Spread on party rye or English muffin halves. Broil until bubbly. Watch carefully. Often I add slices of pepperoni before broiling. I used to buy sharp cheddar cheese in bulk, a five-pound block. I grate part of it in my food processor and freeze in twelve-ounce packages for this recipe. The mixture freezes well too.

I like this fruit cup recipe because it is easy to make, does not need a sweetener, and can be varied easily according to fruit in season. Also, you can make a large or small fruit salad.

Fresh Fruit Cups

2 bananas
1 orange, peeled and cut in small pieces
2 red apples, washed and cored
1 kiwi, peeled and cut into bite-sized pieces
green seedless grapes, approximately 3 cups

Peel and slice bananas; combine with other ingredients and fold together gently with 1 generous tablespoon lemon juice to prevent apples and banana from turning dark or you can use a product called Fruit Fresh as directed on the container. Mix gently. Place in a pretty serving bowl and serve. Makes about 8 servings. Halved strawberries also look nice in this salad! This fruit salad can be served with my recipe for low-fat fruit dip.

Low-Fat Fruit Dip #1

1 cup skim milk
1 cup frozen fat-free whipped topping, thawed
1-3.4-ounce package fat-free instant vanilla pudding mix
3 tablespoons orange juice
1/8 teaspoon almond extract

In a bowl, whisk together milk, pudding mix, orange juice, and almond extract until combined. With spatula, fold in whipped topping until just combined. Transfer to serving bowl; garnish with a mint sprig, if desired. Serve with assorted fresh fruit, such as strawberries, red and green grapes, honeydew, and cantaloupe cubes or my above recipe for fruit salad.

Low-Fat Fruit Dip #2

4 ounces Cool Whip
6 ounces fruit-flavored low-fat yogurt
1 lemonade drink stick or part of a 2-quart
sweetened lemonade package

Blend together and refrigerate. Great on fruit salad or to dip fruit.

This next recipe is from my Amish neighbor, Martha, who is a quiet, hardworking mother of six children. She is a great cook and always available to help when she is needed.

Artichoke Dip

1-14-ounce can artichoke hearts in water
1 cup mayonnaise (I use Hellmann's)
½ cup shredded Parmesan cheese
dash of garlic powder

Drain, then slice artichokes. Combine all ingredients in an ovenproof casserole dish and bake at 350 degrees for 20 minutes. I like this dip spread on oven-crisped slices of French bread.

I found this next recipe in a *Country* magazine a while back. I'm sure this can be made cheaper than the store-bought sauce! We like it very much, since it's quick to make and does make a hard shell on ice cream.

Hard-Shell Ice Cream Sauce

1 cup semisweet chocolate chips
¼ cup butter, cubed
3 tablespoons evaporated milk

In a saucepan, add the chocolate chips, butter, and milk. Heat slowly until chips are melted and the mixture is smooth. The sauce will harden after it's served warm over ice cream,. Refrigerate leftovers. Reheat sauce in microwave. Yields: 1 cup

My daughter Sarah loves hummus. This is a recipe that I found and made for her when she still lived at home, which was about eight years ago so I have since forgotten the source.

Hummus

1-16-ounce can garbanzo beans, drained and liquid reserved
½ cup sesame seeds or ¼ cup tahini (sesame seed paste)
1 clove garlic, cut in half
3 tablespoons lemon juice
1 teaspoon salt
chopped fresh parsley
Pita bread wedges, crackers, or raw vegetables for dipping, if desired

Place reserved bean liquid, the sesame seed paste, and garlic in blender or food processor. Cover and blend on high speed until mixed.

Add beans, lemon juice, and salt. Cover and blend on high speed, stopping blender occasionally to scrape sides if necessary, until uniform consistency.

Spoon dip into serving dish. Garnish with parsley. Serve with pita bread wedges.

My friend Jane gave me the following recipe years ago and it has become a favorite in our household. I make sure I always have it available when we eat hotdogs. Even now that I live in Pennsylvania, I make a supply to take home to my son, Andy, and my sister, Beverly. I make it when green peppers and green tomatoes are in season.

Hot dog Relish

6 green tomatoes or more
6 large green peppers
6 medium to large onions

Grind in medium grinder. Cover with 1/3 cup canning salt and 1 cup water—let sit for 2 hours. Drain and pour cold water over it, then drain again. Mix the following ingredients together and add to the drained vegetables in a large pot.

3 ½ cups sugar
1 teaspoon turmeric
½ cup flour, mixed with 1 ¼ cup vinegar and ¾ cups water

Bring this mixture to a simmer slowly to prevent scorching. Be patient; it takes awhile. I stir frequently with a large wooden spoon.

Cook until thick—seal while hot. Add 1 small jar of

French's yellow prepared mustard last after cooking, just before sealing.

Anyone who has ever planted more than three zucchini seeds needs to have lots of good zucchini recipes on hand for the abundance they will harvest. My now deceased dear friend Hilda gave me this very delicious relish recipe, which is great on hamburgers. I can still hear her saying, "Be sure to use the red peppers not just the green because it makes it prettier."

Hilda's Zucchini Relish

10 cups ground zucchini (with peel on)
4 large onions, ground
4 large sweet green pepper, ground
4 large sweet red peppers, ground
2 ½ cups vinegar
3 cups sugar
1 teaspoon turmeric
2 tablespoons cornstarch
1 teaspoon nutmeg
2 teaspoons celery seed
¼ teaspoon black pepper

Put first four ingredients through a food grinder; sprinkle with ½ cup canning salt. Let stand overnight in a covered container in the refrigerator.

Next morning, drain and rinse well. Mix together with rest of ingredients. Bring to a boil, and then simmer for thirty minutes, being careful not to scorch. Ladle into sterilized jars.

Mom's Easy Sweet Pickle Chips

4 pounds of 3-to 4-inch cucumbers (about 10 cups)
1 quart vinegar
3 tablespoons coarse salt
3 tablespoons mustard seed
¼ cups sugar

Wash cucumbers thoroughly. Cut into ½ to 1-inch chunks. Combine cuke chunks in 1 quart vinegar, salt, mustard seed, and ¼ cup sugar in large saucepan. Simmer covered for 10 minutes. Drain and discard liquid.

Place cucumber chunks in hot sterilized canning jars. Mix:

3½ cups cider vinegar
5 ¾ cups sugar
2 ¼ teaspoons celery seed
1 tablespoon allspice

Mix together in a saucepan. Cook, stirring constantly until sugar is dissolved and mixture reaches boiling point. Fill jars to ⅛ inch from top. Seal at once; process in boiling water bath for 10 minutes. I find that I can use 20 to 30 cups of cucumbers for this amount of liquid.

This icicle pickle recipe is one of my son Chris' favorites. These pickles are very sour. I got this recipe from Mom after I first married. In those days, people in the rural area where I grew up almost always had a dish of pickles or relish on the table at suppertime.

Icicle Pickles

Enough cucumbers for 2 ½ quarts. Slice unpeeled cucumbers lengthwise. Soak in ice water for 2 or 3 hours. Put in jars (quart)—add:

1 tablespoon dry mustard
1 slice onion
1 slice green pepper
Boil:
1 quart cider vinegar
1 cup sugar
½ cup canning salt

Pour over cucumbers and seal in hot, sterilized jars.

I think that my sister Beverly has always used the following bread and butter pickle recipe. She is a good and efficient homemaker. She's also very organized, consistent in whatever she does, and great at knitting and other crafts.

Bev's Bread and Butter Pickles

4 quarts unpared cucumber slices, sliced about ⅛ inch thick, using cucumbers that are not too large
4 small onions, peeled and sliced thin

Place slices in an earthenware or stainless steel bowl. Mix 4 cups cold water with ½ cup pickling salt and pour over slices. Pickling salt does not have cornstarch in it and results in clear brine. It also has better keeping qualities. Let slices stand overnight in brine. Don't put in an aluminum pan.

In the morning, drain and mix with the following ingredients that have been brought to the boiling point:

3 cups sugar
3 cups cider vinegar
1 tablespoon mustard seeds
1 tablespoon celery seeds

Use a large enough pot to bring these to the boiling point. Add drained cucumber and onion slices. Bring back to a boil; cook until cucumber slices are tender, slightly less than fifteen minutes. Have hot, sterilized canning jars ready. Ladle mixture into jars and seal. Makes about 5 pints.

Lynnda's Dill Pickles

Bring to a boil:

1 quart cider vinegar
3 quarts water
1 cup pickling salt
In bottom of each quart jar put:
1 large head dill or 1 teaspoon dill seed
1 large clove garlic
1 teaspoon alum

Pack cucumbers in jars. Cover with liquid and seal.

The following recipe is an easy and attractive finger food recipe to serve at parties! It's convenient because it's best made several hours or even a day before needed.

Easy Tortilla Roll-ups

flour tortillas, 10-inch size
softened cream cheese
thin-sliced boiled ham
dill pickles, sliced length-wise in thin sticks
green onions

Place ham slices on a tortilla, cut ham to fit so as to cover the entire tortilla. With paper towel gently wipe any ham juice off ham; this enables you to spread the softened cream cheese more easily. On top of cream cheese, place thin slices of the pickle at the bottom edge of the tortilla. Roll up the tortilla, starting from the bottom. Wrap each roll in plastic wrap and refrigerate. Continue with the rest of the tortillas. You can use the green onion instead of the pickle as a variation. When needed, slice and place pinwheels on a serving plate. Enjoy!

Clam dip is a New England and family favorite. My son Andy especially loves this and usually is the one that makes it. He thinks it's best with finely chopped onion added in.

Clam Dip

1-8-ounce package cream cheese, softened
1 can minced clams, about 6 ounces
dash of Worcestershire sauce
dash garlic powder

Soften cream cheese, add mostly drained minced clams, and blend well together with a wire whisk. If there is not enough liquid to blend with wire whisk, add a little clam juice or milk to thin. Add Worcestershire sauce, garlic powder, and also minced onion if you prefer.

If you were to read this next recipe through before making it, it seems like it calls for way too much oil; surprisingly however, there is not an oily taste. I used to take these to teen youth group meetings and they were very popular.

Oyster Cracker Munchies

2 packages oyster crackers
2 packages Ranch salad dressing mix (dry)
1 bottle Orville Redenbacher oil

Mix all together. Stir often until oil is absorbed. This won't be greasy even though you use a whole bottle of oil. Make in a large bowl with a tight-fitting cover.

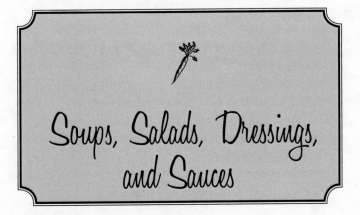

Soups, Salads, Dressings, and Sauces

Poppy Seed Salad Dressing

- ¼ **cup sugar**
- 1 **teaspoon dried, minced onion**
- ¾ **teaspoon poppy seeds**
- ⅛ **teaspoon paprika**
- 2 **tablespoons white wine vinegar**
- 2 **tablespoons cider vinegar**
- ¼ **cup vegetable or olive oil**

Place in a jar, cover and shake well, adding to the salad just before serving. The flavors will blend better if the dressing is made a day ahead.

There are many variations of broccoli salad available, but I like my husband's Uncle Carlton's the best, although I have varied it a little myself.

Broccoli Salad

½ bunch broccoli florets (I use more), washed and drained well
4 slices of bacon, cooked crisp and broken
1 to 2 tablespoons finely chopped onion
¼ cup chopped raisins or dried cranberries
½ cup shredded cheddar cheese
1 tablespoon vinegar
2 tablespoons sugar
½ cup mayonnaise or salad dressing

Mix all and chill. Makes 4–6 servings.

I found this syrup recipe many years ago in a women's magazine and keep it taped to the inside of my kitchen cupboard. I've used it for over twenty-five years at great savings over the store-bought version.

Maple Flavored Syrup

2½ cups water
2½ cups white sugar
2½ cups brown sugar
1½ teaspoons maple flavoring

Combine sugars and water in medium sized saucepan. Bring to boiling, stirring to dissolve sugars. Lower heat and simmer for 5 minutes. Remove from heat; stir in 1½ teaspoons maple flavoring (I use a product called Mapeline) until blended. Store in the refrigerator. We like to heat it in a serving pitcher in the microwave before serving. You can add 3 tablespoons butter or margarine to have butter-flavored syrup. This makes 6 cups of syrup. It keeps well in the refrigerator.

The following recipe is a very flavorful and economical molded salad recipe from an old Albion (my hometown in Maine) cookbook. Except for the orange, I almost always have the other ingredients in my pantry.

Orange Molded Salad

1 small package orange Jell-O
1 cup boiling water

Dissolve together in a four-cup glass mixing bowl. Add:

1 cup crushed pineapple
pulp and juice of 1 orange
½ cup white sugar

Pour into a Jell-O mold. When partially set, add:

½ cup canned evaporated milk, whipped

Place covered in the refrigerator until set. To remove from the mold, set in hot water (up to the rim only) for a few seconds then turn upside down on a serving platter. You might want to run a knife around the edges first to loosen the Jell-O from the sides of the mold if it hasn't pulled away from the mold after placing in hot water.

This next recipe is one that my good friend, Hilda Marr,

used to make. Although she is now deceased, I have great memories of meals we ate in her home.

French Dressing

Beat together for 15 minutes on medium speed:

1 cup ketchup
2 tablespoons vinegar
1 cup salad oil
½ teaspoon garlic salt
¾ cup white sugar
½ teaspoon onion salt

Keep refrigerated.

In the first few months after Steve and I were married, a friend who grew up in a large family gave this recipe to me. She wrote it from memory in my favorite cookbook that is now stained and tattered. I have used this recipe a lot.

Sue's French Dressing

1 can tomato soup
¼ cup vinegar
1–1¼ cups cooking oil
⅓ cup sugar
1 tablespoon Worcestershire sauce
½ teaspoon dry mustard
onion flakes and garlic flakes
¾ teaspoon paprika

Blend well.

The following is another of Sue's economical recipes that I have used regularly for 35 years. I multiply the recipe as needed. It's quick, inexpensive, and always available if tomato paste is kept stocked as a basic pantry staple. I freeze any leftover sauce in a plastic container and add to it each time I make it. Eventually I have enough sauce to defrost and use for a meal of pizza.

Favorite Pizza Sauce

1 6-ounce can tomato paste
1 can water
oregano, red pepper flakes, garlic powder, and sugar (about ½ to 1 teaspoon each) to taste.

Blend with wire whisk. If it seems too thick, add a little more water.

Pork Chop Marinade

½ cup each of soy sauce, water, and honey.

Pour over pork chops and marinate, covered, in the refrigerator overnight. Grill pork chops until done, but don't overcook! Makes enough marinade for 4 pork chops.

This following recipe is one that I developed to make coleslaw dressing, after trying a packaged mix. I liked the flavor, but wanted to be able to make it up with spices from my own kitchen. I didn't want to have to buy the mix when I had the ingredients on hand. In Honduras I wouldn't have been able to find the mix!

Coleslaw

Blend with wire whisk:

1 cup Miracle Whip light or mayonnaise
2 tablespoons sugar
2 tablespoons vinegar
dash of salt and pepper
¼ teaspoon dehydrated onion flakes
1 teaspoon celery seeds

Mix the dressing in with shredded cabbage and finely chopped carrot. Sprinkle top of salad with paprika before serving. This is enough dressing for a large coleslaw!

This is a recipe that my friend June Thompson gave me not long after I got married. It's very easy and tasty!

Bean Salad

1 can green beans
1 can yellow beans
1 can kidney beans
1 cup freshly sliced onion rings
1 cup celery, chopped
1 cup green pepper, chopped

Drain beans well and add celery, onion, and green pepper. Pour hot dressing over all and mix well. Let marinate for several hours or overnight in the refrigerator.

Hot dressing:
Mix together:

½ **cup sugar**
¾ **cup vinegar**
1 teaspoon pepper
½ **cup salad oil**
1 teaspoon salt.

Bring to a boil and pour over beans.

I found this next recipe in a cookbook titled, *Mary Jane's Cookbook*, written by Mary Jane Remole. This is a nice recipe to make ahead, although it's a little sweet.

Mississippi Sunshine Fruit Salad

1 20-ounce can pineapple, drain and save juice
2 unpeeled apples, diced
2 sliced bananas
1 tablespoon lemon juice
1 tablespoon grated orange peel
½ **cup sugar**
⅓ **cup orange juice**
2 tablespoons cornstarch
11-ounce can mandarin oranges, drained

Mix sugar and cornstarch. Blend in lemon juice, orange juice, orange peel and ¾ cup pineapple juice. Bring to a boil. Boil 1 minute stirring constantly. Pour hot mixture over fruit. Refrigerate overnight uncovered. This salad will keep very well!

Praline Ice Cream Sauce

½ cup butter
½ cup whipping cream
1 ½ cups firmly packed light brown sugar
2 tablespoons plus 1 teaspoon light corn syrup
⅓ cup chopped pecans

In a medium saucepan, melt butter; stir in brown sugar and syrup. Bring to a boil. Cook until the sugar is dissolved, stirring constantly. Stir in whipping cream and bring to a boil again. Remove from heat and stir in nuts. Serve warm over ice cream. Store in refrigerator. Makes 2 cups. This is a nice sauce to give as a gift. Simply pour into an attractive jar with a tight fitting lid and tie with a pretty ribbon or raffia. Remember to keep refrigerated!

Pizza Salad is a good recipe when garden tomatoes and green peppers are plentiful. I have had numerous compliments when serving this salad.

Pizza Salad

8 ounces mozzarella or provolone cheese cut into ½ inch cubes
5 tomatoes, seeded and chopped (about 2 ½ pounds)
3 green peppers cut into strips
4 ounces sliced pepperoni
¼ cup chopped onion
1–3 ½ ounce, can pitted ripe olives, optional
½ cup croutons

In a large bowl, combine cheese, tomatoes, green peppers, pepperoni, onion and olives. Add any tomato based salad dressing such as French, Catalina dressing, or the following dressing:

⅓ **cup tomato juice**
¼ **cup vegetable oil**
¼ **cup red wine vinegar**
½ **teaspoon Italian seasoning, crushed**
1 **clove garlic, minced**
1/8 **teaspoon salt**
1/8 **teaspoon pepper**

Combine dressing ingredients by shaking or placing in blender for 30 seconds.

Pour dressing over salad; cover and chill at least 2 hours. Toss before serving. Sprinkle croutons over salad just before serving.

A missionary named Dolly, whom I met at a Bible study while I was living in Honduras, gave me this simple pasta salad recipe. She assured me that this large pasta salad is quick to make, inexpensive and plentiful when having unexpected guests. A pantry salad!

Dolly's Pasta Salad

2 **packages spiral noodles, equivalent to 1-pound box spiral noodles in the U.S.A.**
2 **cans drained tuna**
2 **cans drained canned mixed vegetables. I like a brand that does not contain potato chunks.**

Cook pasta until al dente, drain. Add drained tuna and drained vegetables. Add dried chopped onion or fresh chopped onion as desired. Season as desired, and then add mayonnaise or salad dressing. Refrigerate until cold, and then serve.

My close friend Doreen gave me this recipe that is so quick, kids love it, and I have used it mostly when we have guests.

Easy Molded Salad

1 package raspberry Jell-O
8 ounces boiling water

Mix until Jell-O is dissolved. Add 8-ounce raspberry yogurt. Blend together, then pour in an 8 X 8-inch pan. Chill until firm. You can use any Jell-O and yogurt flavor combinations as desired. Cut into squares when congealed and place on a salad plate. You can garnish with fruit and a dollop of whipped topping.

Tossed Salad with a Different Look

1 head of lettuce; washed, drained and cut into 6 wedges, chilled
1 cup chopped, seeded tomato
1 cup chopped green pepper
1 cup chopped cucumber
8-ounce bottle of French dressing or your choice of your favorite homemade dressing
1 cup corn chips
¼ cup shredded cheddar cheese or cheese of your choice

Combine tomato, green pepper, cucumber and ¼ cup salad dressing; toss lightly. Chill. Arrange chilled lettuce wedge on individual salad plate.

Add corn chips to vegetable mixture; toss lightly. Spoon over lettuce. Top with cheese. Serve with additional dressing as needed. Makes 6 servings.

We like the next salad recipe with or without the chicken. If I want to serve the salad with a main dish I leave out the chicken, however with the chicken it makes a nice main dish served with bread or rolls. This recipe makes enough for 4 servings; adjust the recipe according to how many people you need to serve. The dressing is mild and tastes best if made the day before and refrigerated. Mix the dressing well before adding to the salad.

Caesar Salad with Grilled Chicken

4 boneless, skinless chicken breast halves (about ¾ pound)
Marinade of your choice; I use my homemade recipe or bottled Italian dressing
1 bunch romaine, torn into bite-size pieces
2 tablespoons shredded Parmesan cheese
1 cup seasoned croutons, homemade are best

Marinate chicken at least one hour or overnight. Grill 15 to 20 minutes, turning occasionally, until juices run clear. Cut chicken diagonally into slices.

Toss romaine, cheese, croutons and Caesar dressing. Reassemble chicken breast halves atop salad. Serve with additional grated Parmesan cheese if desired.

Chicken can be broiled instead of grilled. Place boneless, skinless chicken breast halves on rack in broiler pan. Broil with chicken about 4 inches from heat 7 to 8 minutes or until brown. Turn over and broil about 5 minutes longer or until juices run clear.

Caesar dressing:
- ⅓ **cup olive oil**
- 1 **tablespoon lemon juice**
- 1 **tablespoon white wine vinegar**
- 1 **teaspoon Dijon mustard**
- 1 **teaspoon Worcestershire sauce**
- ¼ **teaspoon salt**
- 1 **large clove garlic, crushed**

Place all ingredients in blender. Cover and blend on high speed about 15 seconds or until slightly thickened.

This next salad has no name that I know of. A missionary couple that we visited in a little mountain village in Honduras generously served the salad to us. The hostess said that she often prepares this when she expects company but is not sure when they will arrive. It can be made to serve a lot of people or just a few.

Mrs. Livingston's Salad

- **1–2 pounds hamburger, browned and drained**
- **Chopped tomatoes**
- **Chopped green peppers**
- **Chopped onions**
- **Grated cheddar cheese**
- **Corn chips**

Spicy tomato sauce

Mrs. Livingston told me that she browned the hamburger, drained it than placed it in a Crock-Pot to keep warm. Ahead of time, her maid had chopped the vegetables and placed each type in its own serving dish. A large bag of corn chips was also placed in a large serving bowl (in her situation, it was the local Honduran produced corn chips). She heated the spicy tomato sauce (this was purchased in Honduras, but here in the States you can use prepared taco or enchilada sauce, or even salsa. I would use a homemade taco/enchilada sauce) and pour it into a small serving pitcher.

Place corn chips on a dinner plate, then top with ground beef and chopped vegetables of choice. Pour the warmed sauce over all, then sprinkle with the grated cheese and enjoy! This makes a hearty lunch and goes well with a simple dessert, such as cake or fruit.

I found a variation of this next recipe years ago in a women's magazine. After making a few changes, it has become a real stand by in our home. I use this recipe usually for beef, but occasionally for chicken. It makes tasty, tender London broil or kabobs.

My Favorite Teriyaki Marinade

¼ cup soy sauce
1/8 cup honey
¼ cup red wine vinegar
1 teaspoon minced garlic or garlic powder
¼ cup ketchup
dash of ground ginger

Mix ingredients well in a small bowl, then pour over meat that has been pierced several times with a fork. Marinate for at least 1 hour, turning meat every thirty minutes.

Heat grill or broiler. Cook meat 3–4 inches from heat source. For London broil, cook about 5 minutes per side for rare; 7 minutes for medium; 10 minutes for well done. Slice thinly to serve. Double the recipe when cooking for more than 5 people.

I think it was the first year that *Taste of Home* magazine was published that I submitted this recipe and it was used in their magazine and then their annual cookbook. I recently saw it in their large loose leaf *Taste of Home* cookbook.

Jean's Teriyaki Chicken Marinade

- ¾ **cup soy sauce**
- ½ **teaspoon ginger**
- 3 **tablespoons brown sugar**
- ½ **teaspoon garlic powder**
- 2 **tablespoons sherry**

Shake all ingredients together or blend with wire whisk. Pour marinade over chicken and let marinate from 1 hour to overnight. Using low sodium soy sauce is also very good and less salty.

I developed this chowder recipe from one I had tried, but I felt needed some changes. We like it a lot. It makes a large amount and can be made from pantry items I keep on hand. It would be great to make when camping.

Clam Chowder

**3 cans (6 ½ ounce each) minced or chopped clams,
I like to use Snow's
6 potatoes, washed, peeled and diced
1 large onion, chopped
¼ cup margarine or butter
1 ½ cups water
1 can condensed cream of mushroom soup
1 can condensed cream of celery soup (soups used
in their condensed form)
2—12 ounce cans of evaporated milk
1 teaspoon salt
½ teaspoon pepper**

Drain clams, reserving liquid. Set the clams aside. In a large
pot cook onion in melted margarine or butter until onions
are transparent, being careful not to burn or brown. Add clam
juice, potatoes, water, salt and pepper. Cook over medium
heat for 15 minutes or until potato is tender. Stir in soups,
milk, and clams. Heat through, but be careful not to boil!
Makes 3 quarts, 10 to 12 servings.

Lime Mold

**1 large package lime gelatin mix
1 large package cream cheese, softened
1 small can crushed pineapple, drained
quartered cherries
chopped walnuts**

Dissolve gelatin in 1 cup boiling water and then add 1 cup
cold water. Add softened cream cheese. Beat well with elec-

tric mixer. Add drained crushed pineapple, chopped walnuts, and quartered cherries. Pour into gelatin mold, refrigerate until firm.

Steve's Grandmother Sleeper, who got it from her son in California, gave this next recipe to me. Grammy Sleeper lived in Florida and often made this when we visited. If you do not like sesame seeds or sesame flavor, you will not like this recipe. It is relatively low in fat and probably my favorite chicken salad recipe.

Chinese Chicken Salad

Dressing:

½ cup salad oil
4 tablespoons sugar or sugar substitute equivalent
1 teaspoon pepper
6 tablespoons vinegar

Mix and shake well. This can be made a day ahead, but shake well before serving.

4–6 chicken breasts, cooked and cooled. Use the Microwave Fried Chicken recipe.

1 head lettuce, broken in bite size pieces
4 teaspoons slivered almonds, toasted
2 teaspoons chopped parsley
½ cup finely chopped onions
4 tablespoons toasted sesame seeds

Toss all together; add diced chicken and 1-teaspoon sesame

seed oil. Just before serving, add 1–5 ounce can Chow Mein noodles and salad dressing. Makes a large salad.

Microwave Fried Chicken

For Chinese Chicken Salad

1 cup dried breadcrumbs
1 ½ teaspoons paprika
¼ teaspoon finely crumbled bay leaf
¼ teaspoon garlic powder
½ teaspoon black pepper
1 egg white
1 tablespoon water
¼ cup or less of butter or margarine
4 to 8 boneless, skinless chicken breasts

In bowl, combine breadcrumbs, paprika, salt, bay leaf, garlic powder, and pepper. In another bowl mix egg white with the water. Dip each piece of chicken into the beaten egg white; then coat evenly with the breadcrumb mixture. Place in a round glass-baking dish with larger pieces of chicken on the outside, smaller in the center. In 1 cup glass measuring cup, melt butter in the microwave. Pour over chicken. Cook uncovered about 16 minutes. Let stand 10 minutes before cutting up and adding to salad.

Hot Chicken Salad

2 cups croutons, toasted
¼ cup slivered almonds, toasted
2 cups diced cooked chicken
2 tablespoons minced onion

1 ½ cups chopped celery
½ teaspoon salt
1 ½ cups grated sharp cheese
1 tablespoon lemon juice
¾ cup mayonnaise

Combine half of the croutons with all of the remaining ingredients. Turn into 2-quart baking dish and cover with remaining croutons. Bake at 350 degrees F. for 35 minutes. This may be prepared ahead, but do not add croutons until ready to bake. Serves 6

June's Pink Salad

1 small package cherry Jell-O
1 cup boiling water
½ cup pineapple juice

Chill for ½ hour. Add 1 medium-sized can crushed pineapple. Chill again.

Mix together well:

1-8 ounce package cream cheese
1 cup heavy cream
½ cup walnuts

Mix all together, pour in Jell-O mold and chill until firm. You can substitute low fat cream cheese for regular cream cheese and evaporated skim milk for heavy cream.

Cherry Salad

1 can sweetened condensed milk
1 large container Cool Whip
1-16-ounce can crushed pineapple with juice
1 can cherry pie filling
1 cup chopped nuts or graham cracker crumbs

Mix together milk and Cool Whip, then add remaining ingredients. Pour into a 9" X 13" pan. Freeze 3–4 hours before serving. This would be a good President's Day salad to make for your family. I always liked to serve some kind of cherry dessert on President's Day in memory of George Washington. It would be a fun tradition to start with your children.

Doreen's Peach Salad

1 large (12 ounce) Cool Whip
1 large package peach Jell-O, dry
1 large can peaches, cut-up
½ pint sour cream
miniature marshmallows

You can use whatever fruits you wish and that flavor Jell-O. Blend together and pour into a Jell-O mold. Chill until firm.

Ham Glaze

1 cup brown sugar
½ cup orange juice
½ cup honey

Combine sugar, juice and honey. Remove ham 30 minutes before end of baking time. Remove drippings. Score top of ham in a crisscross pattern, coat ham with glaze. Bake in hot oven (400 degrees F.). Continue to baste ham with the rest of the glaze, in 2 or 3 applications, every 8 to 10 minutes. Do not baste ham with glaze that has run down into drippings as it dulls the luster of the glaze. I use this recipe mainly when I grill a ham steak.

Chocolate Sauce with a Twist

¼ cup cocoa
1 cup of cold water
1 ¾ cups sugar

Cook over medium heat, stirring often. Let boil 3 minutes. Add piece of butter, 1-teaspoon vanilla and a pinch of cinnamon. Steve's mother really liked the cinnamon touch that this recipe has.

Butterscotch Sauce

1 cup light corn syrup
½ cup milk
1 cup light brown sugar
3 tablespoon butter
¼ teaspoon salt
1 teaspoon vanilla

Combine ingredients in saucepan. Cook over medium heat to a full rolling boil and continue cooking for 5 minutes, stirring occasionally. Cool and spoon on servings of cake or ice cream. Be sure not to overcook, as it becomes too hard.

Thick BBQ Sauce

    2 tablespoons butter
    ½ cup cider vinegar
    1 medium onion, chopped
    3 tablespoons honey
    4 cloves garlic, minced
    1 teaspoon soy sauce
    2 tablespoons brown sugar
    ¾ teaspoon Worcestershire sauce
    ¼ teaspoon dry mustard
    6 dashes hot red pepper sauce, optional
    1 can (6 ounce) tomato paste

In saucepan, melt butter over medium heat; sauté onion 4 minutes. Add garlic; sauté 1 minute. Stir in remaining ingredients; boil. Simmer 5 minutes.

When I see the following recipe I think of Easter and my son, Andy. He loves this sauce on ham and used to ask me to double the recipe.

Raisin Ham Sauce

    ½ cup raisins
    few grains salt
    1 ¼ cups water
    2 tablespoons vinegar
    ¼ cup brown sugar
    1 tablespoon margarine

1 tablespoon cornstarch

Combine raisins and water and simmer for 5 minutes. Blend together brown sugar, cornstarch, and salt. Stir into raisins. Cook and stir until clear and slightly thickened. Blend in vinegar and butter. Serve hot. Serves 5 to 6.

Probably 25 years ago I started making the following sauce for ice cream or cake never realizing that it is more commonly called Lemon Curd.

Lemon Dessert Sauce

1 teaspoon grated lemon peel
¼ cup fresh lemon juice
1 cup sugar
6 tablespoons butter or margarine
2 eggs, slightly beaten

In a 1-quart saucepan combine lemon peel and juice, sugar and butter; cook over low heat until butter is melted and sugar is dissolved. Blend a small amount of hot mixture into eggs; return all to saucepan. Cook over medium heat, stirring constantly, until mixture thickens slightly. Do not boil. Cool. Makes 1 ½ cups sauce.

The following recipe for pizza sauce is very good, but I usually use a simpler version.

Pizza Sauce

1 tablespoon olive oil
1 ½ teaspoon sugar

1 medium onion, diced
1 teaspoon Italian herb seasoning
1 garlic clove, minced
¼ teaspoon crushed red pepper
1-16-ounce can tomatoes
1 teaspoon salt
1-6-ounce can tomato paste

In a 2-quart saucepan over medium heat, in 1 tablespoon hot oil, cook onion and garlic until tender. Add tomatoes with their liquid, tomato paste, sugar, herb seasoning, red pepper, and salt; heat to boiling, stirring to break up tomatoes. Reduce heat to low; cover partially and simmer 20 minutes. Cool.

The following recipe makes a quick, easy, and colorful accompaniment to any holiday or company meal. This can also be used as a dessert. Top each serving with whipped topping and garnish with chopped nuts and maybe a sprig of mint leaves! It's a nice salad or dessert to serve on St. Patrick's Day because of its green color. I used to like to serve some green foods on that holiday because the kids thought it was fun.

Pistachio Pudding Salad

1-16-ounce container whipped topping
1 large can crushed pineapple
1 cup miniature marshmallows
½ cup chopped nuts, optional
1-6-ounce package instant pistachio pudding mix

In a large bowl stir whipped topping until smooth. Add marshmallows (colored look nice) and pudding mix. Stir in pineapple with juice and nuts. Refrigerate at least 1 hour. This makes a large amount.

Easy Pantry Fruit Salad

1-20-ounce can pineapple chunks in juice
1-11-ounce can drained mandarin oranges
2 sliced bananas
1-16-ounce can fruit cocktail with juice
1-3¾-ounce package instant lemon pudding mix

In a medium bowl, combine pineapple chunks and juice with bananas, mandarin oranges, and fruit cocktail with juice. Stirring slowly, sprinkle pudding mix into fruit mixture. Let stand 5 minutes. The pudding will set in the fruit juice. This makes about 6½ cups or 13 ½ cup servings.

At one of our favorite restaurants in Honduras, I always ordered a chicken salad with hot bacon dressing. This recipe is as close as I can get to that salad dressing.

Hot Bacon Dressing

¾ pound sliced bacon, diced
2 tablespoons Dijon mustard
½ cup chopped onion
1 teaspoon salt
1 cup cider vinegar
¼ teaspoon pepper
2 cups water
3 tablespoons cornstarch
1½ cups sugar
2 tablespoons cold water

In a large skillet, cook bacon until crisp; remove bacon and set aside. Drain, reserving 2 tablespoons drippings in the skillet. Add onion and sauté until tender; remove from heat. Add the vinegar, water, sugar, mustard, salt, pepper, and bacon; mix well. Combine cornstarch and cold water; stir into skillet. Cook and stir until mixture comes to a boil. Boil for 2 minutes, stirring constantly. Serve warm over fresh salad. Refrigerate leftovers and reheat before serving. Makes about 4 cups.

My mother's good friend, Ginny, gave me the following recipe for cocktail sauce back in 1970. It's nice to be able to make this from pantry ingredients when you need it and don't have a jar of it on hand.

Cocktail Sauce for Seafood

½ cup ketchup
3 drops Tabasco sauce, if desired
1 tablespoon prepared horseradish
1 tablespoon lemon juice, if desired
½ teaspoon Worcestershire sauce
1½ teaspoons brown sugar
¼ teaspoon salt
½ teaspoon onion juice, if desired

Blend together with wire whisk; chill well. This makes about ¾ cup of sauce.

Homemade Tartar Sauce

Mix together mayonnaise or Miracle Whip with green sweet hamburger relish according to your taste and the amount you will need. Let sit about an hour before using to blend flavors.

I used to bake fish sticks in a baking pan for the family when the kids were young. To make them a little more special, I would spread them with a thin layer of homemade tarter sauce, place slices of American cheese on top, then bake as directed. I think this is something my friend and co-worker Betty Mason taught me.

Fish Chowder

- **¼ pound salt pork or 3 tablespoons butter**
- **1 teaspoon salt**
- **2 onions, sliced or diced**
- **¼ teaspoon pepper**
- **4 cups potatoes, cut into small pieces**
- **2 or 3 cups whole milk**
- **1 or 2 cups water**
- **1-12-ounce can evaporated milk**
- **2 pounds fish fillets (we like Icelandic haddock)**

Fry diced salt pork slowly in bottom of heavy pot until golden colored; if using butter, melt slowly. Remove pork scraps and set aside. There should be about 3 tablespoons fat in the pot. Add onions and cook until yellowed (but not brown). Add potatoes and enough water so it comes nearly to top of potatoes. Place fish on top of potatoes, sprinkle with seasonings. Cover, bring to a boil, then cook on low heat until potatoes are tender and the fish flakes. Pour in both kinds of milk and allow to heat thoroughly without boiling. The chowder is ready when it is heated through. Makes 6 servings. Stir soup gently so as not to break up fish, which could make it mushy. Chowders always taste better the second day!

Maine Corn Chowder

2 tablespoons margarine
1 cup water
1 small diced onion
2 cans cream style corn
3 cups peeled and diced raw potatoes
3 cups whole milk
2 teaspoons salt
1-12-ounce can evaporated milk
¼ teaspoon pepper

Use a good-sized pot. Place 2 teaspoons margarine in the pan. Melt over low heat then add 1 small diced onion and cook slowly until onion is transparent, being careful not to brown or burn. Add water, diced raw potato, salt, and pepper. Cover and bring to steaming point. Lower heat and cook until potato is tender, about 15 minutes. Add corn and both kinds of milk. Taste for seasoning. You may add a piece of margarine, but it's not really needed. Reheat slowly. Allow chowder to ripen for an hour to develop flavor. Ripen is an old cooking term we use in New England, meaning to bring out the flavor. You do this by letting it set on low heat just to keep it warm, letting the flavors blend together. Don't boil a soup that has a milk base. Makes 4 generous servings.

Hamburger and Vegetable Soup

3 tablespoons butter
½ teaspoon black pepper
¾ pound hamburger
3 carrots, sliced
3 onions, sliced
3 potatoes, peeled and diced
3 stalks celery, diced
⅓ cup barley
1 teaspoon Worcestershire sauce
2½ cups canned tomatoes
1½ quarts water
2 teaspoons salt

Using a large soup pot, brown meat in a small amount of oil. Crumble so that the meat is separated. Add onions and cook for a few minutes longer. Add water, tomatoes, barley, salt, and pepper. Cover and simmer gently over low heat for 1 hour.

Add vegetables and Worcestershire; bring back to steaming point, lower heat and cook for another hour. Makes 6 large helpings. I like to add cheese dumplings when the soup is done.

Cheese Dumplings

2 cups homemade biscuit mix
1 cup shredded cheddar cheese
⅔ cup milk

Mix together until moist. Drop a tablespoonful on hot soup until all dough is used. Place cover on pan and simmer for 12 minutes. Don't lift cover until after the 12-minute cooking time.

Crock-Pot Chicken Soup

Depending on the size of your Crock-Pot, take 1 or 2 chicken carcasses or a half turkey carcass and the night before you want the chicken soup, place the carcass or carcasses in your Crock-Pot. Fill the Crock-Pot with water to cover carcass. Add some salt, pepper, and poultry seasoning, a couple of bay leaves, 2 or 3 chicken bouillon cubes, and some celery tops. Cover and cook all night on low. In the morning take out the bones, celery, and bay leaves, discard. Next, skim off the fat. Add chopped celery, onions, and sliced carrots to the pot. Season as needed to taste. If you have any extra cut-up chicken on hand you can add that to the chicken bits already in the soup from the carcass. You can add barley or rice at this time, as well as any leftover vegetables that you would like. Cook on low all day. One half hour before serving, add dry noodles to the soup if desired. When the noodles are ready, so is the soup! Sometimes if we did not want a soup meal right away after baking chickens or a turkey, I would freeze the carcass and some leftover chicken or turkey and label "for soup."

Warm Blueberry Sauce

2 tablespoons water
1½ cups Maine blueberries
½ teaspoon cornstarch
2 tablespoons sugar
2 teaspoons fresh lemon juice

In a 1-quart saucepan, combine water, cornstarch, 1½ cups blueberries, and 2 tablespoons sugar. Heat to boiling over medium heat, stirring occasionally. Boil 1 to 2 minutes or until berries burst. Remove from heat; stir in lemon juice.

My daughter-in-law Stacy gave me her favorite recipe for hot fudge sauce that her mom, Ginger had given to her. It is very good!

Ginger's Hot Fudge Sauce

In a double boiler, melt together 2 squares unsweetened chocolate and ¼ cup butter.

Add ⅛ teaspoon salt and 1½ cups sugar to melted mixture. Slowly blend in 1 cup and 2 tablespoons evaporated milk. Stir until thick, about ½ hour. Add 1 teaspoon vanilla after cooking. This sauce is nice and rich and thick. Great over ice cream! Store in the refrigerator.

Main Dishes

The following recipe is very similar to the Outback Steakhouse's Alice Springs Chicken. I think I first made it from a recipe found in one of the Reiman publications.

Bacon-Cheese Topped Chicken

½ cup Dijon mustard
4½ teaspoons canola oil, divided
½ cup honey
½ teaspoon lemon juice
4 boneless, skinless chicken breast halves
¼ teaspoon salt
dash paprika
⅛ teaspoon fresh ground pepper
2 cups sliced fresh mushrooms
2 tablespoons butter
1 cup (4 ounces) shredded Jack cheese
1 cup (4 ounces) shredded cheddar cheese
8 bacon strips, partially cooked
2 teaspoons minced fresh parsley

Combine the mustard, honey, and 1½ teaspoon oil and

lemon juice in a bowl. Pour ½ cup marinade into a large resealable plastic bag, then add chicken. Seal and turn to coat chicken, then refrigerate for 2 hours. Cover and refrigerate the remaining marinade.

Drain and discard marinade from chicken. In a large skillet over medium heat, brown chicken in remaining oil on all sides then sprinkle chicken with salt, pepper, and paprika. Place chicken in a greased 11" x 7" x 2" baking dish.

In the same skillet, sauté mushrooms in butter until tender. Spoon reserved marinade over chicken and top with cheeses and mushrooms. Place bacon strips in a crisscross pattern over chicken. Bake, uncovered, at 375 degrees for 20–25 minutes or until meat thermometer reads 160 degrees. Sprinkle with parsley. Makes 4 servings.

Wake-up casserole is a recipe that my daughter-in-law Stacy gave to me. She is an excellent cook and says that she usually makes this on Christmas morning for her family.

Wake-Up Casserole

8 rectangle hash brown patties, thawed
2 cups shredded cheddar cheese
2 cups fully cooked ham cubes

Grease a 9" x 13" baking dish. Place one layer of hash brown patties on the bottom, then layer the cheese and ham. This can be done the night before!

In the morning, beat together:

7 eggs
1 cup milk

½ **teaspoon salt**
½ **teaspoon dry mustard**

Pour over other ingredients in baking dish. Cover tightly with aluminum foil and bake for 1 hour at 350 degrees. Remove the foil and bake another 15 minutes until brown. Test for doneness.

I believe this breakfast recipe is one my sister Bev uses. It is very good.

Breakfast Casserole

6 eggs
1 pound ground sausage
2 cups milk
2 slices bread, cubed
1 teaspoon salt
1 cup shredded cheddar cheese
1 teaspoon dry mustard

Butter a 9"x 9" baking dish. Cover the bottom with the bread cubes. Cook sausage; drain. Sprinkle over the bread cubes, then sprinkle cheddar cheese over sausage. Beat together the eggs, milk, salt, and dry mustard; pour over the above mixture. Cover and refrigerate overnight. Bake 35 to 40 minutes at 350 degrees.

Broccoli and Cheese Casserole

2-10-ounce boxes chopped broccoli
1 cup shredded sharp cheddar cheese

1 cup shredded mozzarella cheese
37 Ritz crackers, crushed

Layer the ingredients in a greased casserole dish, ending with the cheese on top. Add 2 pats of margarine. Pour 1½ cups of milk over the entire mixture. Bake at 350 degrees for 1 hour.

Broccoli Cauliflower Casserole

1-10¾-ounce can cream of celery or chicken soup, undiluted
1-8-ounce jar processed cheese spread
1-10-ounce package frozen, chopped broccoli
1-10-ounce package frozen, chopped cauliflower
1-2.8-ounce can French fried onions

In a bowl, combine soup and cheese. Add broccoli and cauliflower. Spoon into a greased 2-quart baking dish. Top with onions and bake uncovered, at 350 degrees for 25 to 30 minutes.

I remember Mom cooking pork chops with mushroom gravy when I was growing up and often used this recipe myself. I don't think this recipe has ever been written down before this.

Mom's Pork Chops

Brown pork chops in cast iron frying pan. When both sides are lightly browned, add 1 can cream of mushroom soup blended with about ¼ cup milk. Turn down the heat, cover, and let simmer until the pork chops are thoroughly cooked.

Enjoy! This is not a low-fat dish! Low-fat cream of mushroom soup can be used instead of the regular cream of mushroom soup.

Stromboli

The ingredients are for 1 loaf of dough. If using frozen bread dough, defrost and let rise at room temperature. Stretch and pat into a rectangle that measures approximately 11" x 13".

Filling:

Use approximately ¼ pound sliced pepperoni, ¼ pound thin sliced provolone, and 1 small can mushrooms, chopped.

Beat 1 to 2 eggs with salt, pepper, oregano, garlic powder, and Parmesan cheese. With pastry brush, coat entire piece of flattened dough with egg mixture, then layer with pepperoni, overlapping the pieces. Lay the slices of provolone cheese over the pepperoni, then sprinkle the mushrooms on top.

Roll the dough as you would a jellyroll. Brush the top and sides with the egg mixture. Place loaf on a greased cookie sheet and bake in a preheated oven at 350 degrees until brown. You can substitute sliced ham and Swiss cheese for the pepperoni and provolone.

Marinated Chicken Wings

5 pounds chicken wings
8 ounces soy sauce
8 ounces honey
½ teaspoon garlic powder

Marinate chicken wings, soy sauce, honey, and garlic powder overnight. Bake the wings for 1 hour at 350 degrees, turning once and applying more marinade.

Stir Fry Chicken and Vegetables

Teriyaki Sauce:
6 ounces soy sauce
2 tablespoons cooking sherry
3 tablespoons brown sugar
½ teaspoon ground ginger
½ teaspoon garlic powder

Blend all ingredients well. Cut up boneless chicken into bite-sized pieces and place in a zipper type bag or baking dish. Pour teriyaki sauce over chicken. Marinate chicken for 1 hour, turning to coat well about every 15 minutes.

Cut up at least 5 to 6 cups of raw vegetables such as celery, onions, green pepper, carrots, mushrooms, broccoli, or whatever you have available.

Stir-fry chicken in about 1 teaspoon oil until done, stirring continuously, using high heat in wok. When the chicken is cooked, remove to a bowl. Add 1 to 2 teaspoons oil to wok; add cut-up vegetables, stirring until crisp-tender, approximately 5 minutes on high heat. Add cooked chicken to vegetables. Sprinkle with soy sauce, then cover and remove from heat. Let stand approximately 5 minutes. Serve over white rice. Chopped green onion on the top adds an attractive and flavorful touch.

Steve's sister, Sandi, used to make the following casserole

often at holiday get-togethers. It does not cook well in a small Crock-Pot; she used a 4-quart size. It is a hearty casserole!

Company Casserole

1¼ cups raw converted rice
½ cup melted butter or margarine
2½ to 3 cups chicken broth
3 to 4 cups cut-up, cooked chicken
2-4-ounce cans sliced mushrooms, drained
⅓ cup soy sauce
1-12-ounce package frozen, shelled salad shrimp
8 green onions, chopped

Mix rice with melted butter or margarine in Crock-Pot. Stir to coat rice thoroughly. Add all remaining ingredients. Cover and cook on low 6 to 8 hours or on high for 3 to 4 hours.

Sloppy Joe Recipe #1

1 pound lean ground beef
2 beef flavor bouillon cubes
½ cup chopped green pepper
2 teaspoons sugar
½ cup chopped onion
1 teaspoon prepared mustard
1 cup ketchup
¼ cup water
4 hamburger rolls, split and toasted

In skillet, brown meat with pepper and onion and then pour off the fat. Add remaining ingredients except hamburger buns; bring to a boil. Reduce heat; cover and simmer 15 to 20 minutes. Serve on buns. Refrigerate leftovers. Serves 4.

Sloppy Joe Recipe #2

Brown: **1 pound hamburger**
1 small minced onion
Add:
½ cup ketchup
2 teaspoons mustard
2 tablespoons brown sugar
1 teaspoon Worcestershire sauce
2 tablespoons vinegar
1 teaspoon salt

Simmer for 20 minutes. This makes enough for 4 Sloppy Joe sandwiches. It's thicker than some sauces. My husband likes this recipe better than Sloppy Joe Recipe #1.

Corny casserole is a variation of American chop suey; however, I think this is more flavorful. My friend Linda Gillette gave me this recipe many years ago and I have used it a lot.

Corny Casserole

¼ cup chopped onion
1 tablespoon soy sauce
1½ pounds ground beef
1-16-ounce can stewed tomatoes
2 tablespoons cooking oil
1½ teaspoons salt
1-16-ounce can whole kernel corn
⅛ teaspoon pepper

¼ teaspoon crushed, dried basil
1 cup uncooked macaroni

Cook macaroni until al dente, drain and place in a large, greased casserole dish. In frying pan, add oil and chopped onion; cook until onions are transparent, but not burned. Brown ground beef, drain off any fat. Add drained corn, undrained tomatoes, soy sauce, and spices. Heat until bubbly, then pour over cooked macaroni in casserole dish. Mix well and top with grated cheddar or Parmesan cheese. Bake at 350 to 400 degrees until bubbly, approximately 35 to 45 minutes.

This recipe can be varied. Sometimes I add more macaroni, eliminate the stewed tomatoes, add 1 6-ounce can tomato paste, 1 soup can water and a can of tomato soup. Also, I always eliminate the cooking oil and spray the frying pan with a nonstick spray instead.

My good friend Doreen Marr gave me the following recipe several years ago. It is a good recipe to make for company and a great recipe to use up leftover turkey from Thanksgiving or Christmas. We often had this dish at Doreen's parents' house in Maine during the Christmas season.

Chicken Divan

2-10-ounce packages frozen broccoli or 2 bunches fresh broccoli, chopped or spears
3 cups sliced, cooked chicken or turkey
2-10½-ounce cans of cream of chicken soup
1 cup mayonnaise, salad dressing does not work in this recipe
2 tablespoons lemon juice

¾ **cup grated sharp cheese**
3 cups soft breadcrumbs in 2 tablespoons melted margarine

Cook broccoli in boiling water. Arrange broccoli in greased 9" x 13" baking dish. Place chicken on top. Combine soup, mayonnaise, and lemon juice; pour over chicken. Sprinkle with grated cheese and spread breadcrumbs over all. Bake 25 to 30 minutes at 350 degrees.

Holiday Rice

1 cup long grain white rice
1 can beef consommé
¼ **cup melted margarine**
1 can beef bouillon
1 small onion, chopped
1 small can mushrooms, drained

Place all ingredients in a greased casserole dish. Cover and bake 1 to 1½ hours in a 350-degree oven.

Fajitas—Chicken or Beef

1½ pounds boneless steak strips or 4 boneless, skinless chicken breast halves
¼ **cup red wine vinegar**
1 teaspoon sugar
1 teaspoon dried oregano leaves
1 teaspoon chili powder
½ **teaspoon garlic powder**
½ **teaspoon salt or less**
¼ **teaspoon pepper**

10 large flour tortillas
2 large onions, sliced
2 red and/or green sweet peppers, cut into thin strips
1 jar picante sauce or salsa

Trim fat off beef or chicken. Marinate meat in first seven ingredients for at least 1 hour. Stir-fry meat in a wok or frying pan in 1 scant tablespoon of olive oil. When cooked, place in a serving bowl and keep warm. Stir-fry onions and peppers until soft. I add a dash of soy sauce. Add meat after vegetables are cooked. Heat tortilla shells. Wrap meat mixture in warm shells, add salsa, and enjoy!

Years ago, when Chris was a young teenager, he had chicken cordon bleu at a local restaurant. It wasn't possible to take the whole family there very often because it was too expensive. I experimented with a few recipes and the following is the result of that. We all like it a lot at our house; however, it is not a low-calorie dish.

We recently made this dish when my daughter, Sarah, and her family were visiting. We set the table with a black-and-gold-colored tablecloth, tied white cloth napkins with wide black grosgrain ribbon, had an Eiffel tower centerpiece with a candle, and played French music in the background. We all really enjoyed the atmosphere and dinner. The tablecloth and ribbon were from a ribbon factory outlet that together cost under $5. The tablecloth fabric was very elegant with its embossing in gold thread. The Eiffel tower centerpiece cost under $15 and the CD of French music came with some recipes and was only $1.

Chicken Cordon Bleu

4 whole boneless, skinless chicken breasts
8 thin slices ham
8 cubes Swiss cheese
1 cup shredded Swiss cheese
Sauce:
4–6 tablespoons butter or margarine
6 tablespoons flour
½ teaspoon dried, crushed thyme leaves
2 cups chicken broth (4 teaspoons instant chicken
bouillon granules, dissolved in 2 cups hot water)
1 cup milk
salt and pepper to taste

Melt margarine in saucepan. Stir in flour and thyme, then blend in broth and milk. Cook, stirring until sauce thickens. Season to taste with salt and pepper.

Cut each chicken breast into 2 halves. Pound each half breast between waxed paper until ½ inch thick.

Roll ham and cheese cube in each chicken breast half. Secure with toothpicks. Dip in beaten egg or egg whites and coat with fine breadcrumbs. Lightly brown coated breasts in margarine or butter in frying pan over medium heat, being careful not to burn. Place each breast in greased 9" x 13" baking pan, removing toothpicks before baking. Pour sauce over breasts, then sprinkle with shredded Swiss cheese. Bake in 400-degree oven for 40 minutes.

Quick Quiche

1½ cups milk
¼ cup melted margarine or butter
2 eggs
½ cup Bisquick or homemade biscuit mix

Sprinkle 1 cup grated cheddar cheese (or your choice of cheese) in the bottom of a 10-inch pie plate. Next, place cooked ground beef, chopped cooked chicken, or 1 can drained shrimp over cheese. Add about 1 cup of al dente cooked vegetables, such as broccoli and cauliflower pieces.

Blend milk, eggs, butter, and dry biscuit mix in blender or food processor until well blended, then pour over cheese, meat, and vegetables in pie plate. Bake at 375 degrees for about 40 minutes, or until knife inserted in middle comes out clean.

My mother-in-law gave me the following quiche Lorraine recipe not long after I was married. I continue to use it, as I think it is the best recipe that I have tried. I sometimes add ham, broccoli, cauliflower, shrimp, or a combination of these instead of bacon.

Quiche Lorraine

1-9-inch unbaked pie shell
1½ cups medium all-purpose cream
½ pound sliced bacon
¾ teaspoon salt
1½ cups grated Swiss cheese (6 ounces)
dash nutmeg
dash pepper

3 eggs

Prepare pie shell and refrigerate until ready to use. Preheat oven to 375 degrees. Fry bacon until crisp, drain. Crumble into bits and sprinkle over bottom of prepared pie shell. Sprinkle grated cheese over bacon. Beat eggs with cream, salt, and spices until well combined, but not frothy. Pour over cheese into pie shell. Bake 35 to 40 minutes, or until top is golden and center seems firm when gently shaken. Let quiche cool on wire rack for 10 minutes before serving. Sometimes I eliminate the bacon and add cooked vegetables and cooked shrimp.

Baked Beef Stew

2 pounds stew beef
2 stalks celery, cut up
1 envelope dry onion soup mix
6 carrots, cut up
1 can cream of mushroom soup
1 can cream of celery soup
5 potatoes, peeled and cut up
¼ -½ cup water (do not add the water if cooking in a Crock-Pot)
1 tablespoon Worcestershire sauce

Spread a layer of stew meat in a 9" x 13" pan. Sprinkle with dry onion soup mix and add other soups and Worcestershire sauce. Add layer of vegetables and pour water over all. Cover with foil and bake at 300 degrees for 5 hours. Don't peek, that is the secret!

If cooking in a Crock-Pot, place vegetables on the bottom,

then meat. Pour soups over all. Eliminate the water. Cook on low for 12 hours.

Stay-A-Bed Stew

2 pounds browned stew beef
peeled carrots, onions, celery, green pepper, and peeled potatoes, all cut in fairly large-sized chunks

Place all in a greased 9" x 13" inch pan. Use 1 or 2 cans of diluted tomato soup. Pour over meat and vegetables. Sprinkle ½ package beef stew seasoning over all. Cover tightly with aluminum foil. Bake at 350 degrees for 2 hours or more. For the last ½ hour of baking, add a can of drained string beans or peas. This is very good!

The following chicken and rice casserole has to be one of the easiest and most economical casserole recipes that I have. I think my friend Debbie Hamlin gave it to me many years ago when our children were little.

Chicken and Rice Casserole

1 envelope onion soup mix
1 can cream of mushroom soup
1 cup raw, white rice
1½ cups hot water
cut up chicken parts

Mix ingredients together and pour into a greased 9" x 13" baking pan. Over this mixture, place cut-up chicken parts. Sprinkle with paprika and parsley flakes. Cover tightly with aluminum foil and bake for 1½ hours at 400 degrees.

Bacon and Bean Casserole

8 strips bacon
2-1-pound cans baked beans
3 tablespoons brown sugar
2 teaspoons dry mustard
3 tablespoons molasses

Preheat oven to 350 degrees. Pour beans into a casserole dish. Cut 3 strips of bacon into small pieces, then add to beans along with molasses, brown sugar, and dry mustard. Mix well. Cut remaining bacon strips in half and place on top of bean mixture. Do not cover. Bake 30 to 35 minutes or until the bacon looks cooked. Makes 4 servings.

Oven-Fried Rice

2 cups uncooked rice
1 cup finely chopped celery
3¼ cups cold water
1 small can drained mushrooms
1 envelope onion soup mix
1 can bean sprouts, drained
½ cup soy sauce
⅓ cup vegetable oil
cooked cubed ham, beef, or chicken, optional

Sauté the celery in small amount of margarine in microwave until soft (I usually omit this step). Combine all ingredients in a thick pan or roaster pan. Bake covered at 350 degrees for 1¼ hours. Stir rice only when you take out of the oven. Easy. Fills a 9" x 13" pan.

Crock-Pot instructions: Cook for 45 to 60 minutes on high, then on low for 3 ½ hours.

Tater Tot Casserole

1 pound lean uncooked ground beef
1 can cream of mushroom soup
2 tablespoons chopped onion (fresh or dried)
1-pound package frozen potato puffs

Crumble raw hamburger loosely into an 8" x 8" or 11" x 7" pan. Sprinkle with chopped onion. Spread undiluted soup over all. Place frozen potato puffs in rows across the whole pan. Bake uncovered for 1 hour at 375 degrees. Makes 5 or 6 servings.

Simple Tuna Casserole

1 can drained tuna
½ cup cooked peas
1 can cream of mushroom soup
½ cup crushed potato chips

Mix all together and pour into casserole dish. Use some extra crushed potato chips on the top. Double or triple as needed. Bake at 350 degrees until bubbly.

Oven Spanish Rice

1 to 2 tablespoons butter or margarine
1-16-ounce can stewed tomatoes
1 small onion, chopped

¼ cup chopped green pepper

Place butter, onion, and green pepper into a casserole dish. Microwave on high until vegetables are soft. Add enough water to the stewed tomatoes to equal 2 to 2 ¼ cups. Bring to a boil in the microwave on high. Add 1 teaspoon salt, ⅛ teaspoon black pepper and 1 cup of raw white rice.

Bake in a 350-degree oven for 35 minutes. Fluff with fork after 15 minutes.

Easy Chicken Parmangiana

8 skinless, boneless chicken breast halves
2 egg whites
1 tablespoon water
approximately 2 tablespoons butter or margarine
fine bread crumbs, plain or Italian
1-32-ounce jar spaghetti sauce
1 cup mozzarella cheese
parmesan cheese

Dip each chicken breast half in a mixture of 2 beaten egg whites and 1 tablespoon water. Coat with fine breadcrumbs regular or Italian flavored. Brown both sides of chicken breasts in melted butter, then place in greased baking pan. Pour 1 jar of your favorite spaghetti sauce over chicken. Sprinkle with shredded mozzarella cheese. Next, sprinkle with Parmesan cheese. Bake at 400 degrees for about 20 minutes, or until juices from chicken run clear.

The following chicken and stuffing casserole that I developed is similar to others that I have seen. I used to take this to potluck meals. It is hearty, tasty, and looks nice. I like Swiss cheese with chicken better than other types of cheeses.

Chicken and Stuffing Casserole

1-16-ounce package of Pepperidge Farm stuffing mix, prepared as directed.

Set aside 1 or 1 ½ cups of prepared stuffing. Press the remainder of the stuffing mixture in the bottom and up the sides of a greased 9" x 13" baking pan. I like to use a glass baking pan for this recipe. Using 4 whole boneless, skinless chicken breasts, cook and cut up into bite-sized pieces.

With a wire whisk, mix together:

1 can cream of chicken soup
1 can cream of celery soup
⅔ cup evaporated milk
⅓ cup water
1 tablespoon flour

Combine with cut-up chicken. Pour into stuffing-lined pan. Sprinkle leftover stuffing over the top, followed by ⅓ to ½ cup shredded Swiss cheese. Sprinkle all with seasoned salt and a dash of black pepper. Bake at 400 degrees for about 30 minutes, or until hot in the middle and bubbly around the sides.

We like the following chili recipe in our home, since we like the meat more than the beans. We often double or triple the recipe. Usually we add the kidney beans, but sometimes we leave them out. My son Andy has made this recipe a lot!

Quick Chili

1 pound ground beef
2 teaspoons chili powder
1 small onion, chopped
1 teaspoon salt
1-6-ounce can tomato paste
12 ounces water
½ teaspoon cumin, optional
¼ teaspoon black pepper
1 to 2 tablespoons brown sugar
1-16-ounce can kidney beans, rinsed and drained
shredded cheddar cheese

In a saucepan, brown beef and onion. Drain fat. Stir in all remaining ingredients except cheese; cover and simmer 20 minutes. Top each serving with cheese, if desired. Makes 4 servings. Instead of simmering for 20 minutes, this can be made ahead and placed in a Crock-Pot and left on low all day.

My daughter Sarah has been married for 6 years and she is acquiring some of her husband's family's tried and true recipes. The following is the chili recipe that she and Andrew like a lot.

Neill Chili

1 pound hamburger
1 chopped onion
Cook and drain. Add:
2 cans tomato soup
1 teaspoon cumin

2 cans kidney beans
1 teaspoon salt
1 large can crushed tomatoes
1 teaspoon sugar
1 tablespoon crushed chili powder
½ teaspoon garlic powder

Cook and drain the hamburger and onion, then combine with the remaining ingredients. Simmer until thick.

I really like this recipe for Chinese chicken wings. The red color reminds me of authentic Chinese pork or chicken wings.

Chinese Chicken Wings

24 chicken wings
2 teaspoons garlic powder
3 tablespoons soy sauce
2 tablespoons sugar
2 tablespoons cooking sherry
½ teaspoon red food coloring

Remove wing tips. Combine ingredients and marinate wings in mixture 6 hours or overnight. Remove from mixture and bake in 350-degree oven for 1 hour. Marinade can also be used on pork spare ribs.

The following enchilada recipe is one that I developed to use pantry items rather than buying another type of sauce for the pantry shelf. I always have seasonings and tomato paste on hand. I like to keep flour tortillas on hand since they are so versatile. Just a few uses include appetizer roll-ups, enchiladas, wrap sandwiches and chicken and cheese quesadillas. The tortillas keep for a long time once the package is open by storing them in the refrigerator. Tortillas also freeze well; however, if frozen for more than a couple of months they become dry and flaky after thawing.

Jean's Enchiladas

1 package taco seasoning mix (See my recipe for taco seasoning mix.)
1-6-ounce can tomato paste
1¾ cups water
8 ounces shredded cheddar cheese
1 package 10-inch flour tortilla shells
1¼ pounds hamburger

Brown hamburger and drain. Combine taco seasoning mix, tomato paste, and water; mix well with wire whisk. Combine drained, cooked hamburger with half of sauce mixture and half of shredded cheddar cheese. To cause the tortillas to be crisp without deep frying, I place two on a baking sheet in a very hot oven just until they puff up, without becoming crisp. I then turn them over and puff the other side. Watch carefully to prevent burning or crisping. This step can be omitted if you prefer. Put a generous tablespoon of mixture on lower end of tortilla and roll up, placing seam-side down in a greased 9" x 13" glass baking dish. When all tortillas are filled and placed in a baking pan, pour the remaining sauce down the center of the tortillas, then sprinkle with remaining shredded cheddar cheese. Bake at 350 degrees for about 25 minutes uncovered.

Kristina lived with us for six months last year. Her mother

moved to Texas, and Kristina wanted to finish her senior year of high school and her freshman year in college (both in the same semester) here in Pennsylvania. We enjoyed doing this as a ministry and she blessed us. Her grandparents are originally from Mexico so she enjoys making and eating Mexican food. The recipe she wrote out for me is what her grandparents passed down to her, apparently never written before. These enchiladas do taste more authentic than mine.

Kristina's Enchiladas

- **1½ pounds cooked hamburger**
- **1½ pounds shredded cheddar cheese**
- **2-8-count packages yellow corn tortillas**
- **2-19-ounce cans enchilada sauce**
- **2 tablespoons chili powder**
- **2 tablespoons dried onion flakes**

Preheat oven to 400 degrees. Use a 9" x 13" pan. Mix the chili powder, onion flakes, and sauce, thickening with a little flour if desired. Cover the bottom of the pan with some of the sauce. Dip the corn tortillas in the sauce. Roll a little bit of the meat and cheese into the tortilla. Place inside pan, repeating until the pan is full. Sprinkle remaining ingredients on top. Cover with aluminum foil and bake for about 20 minutes.

Baked Spanish Rice

- **1-28-ounce can crushed tomatoes in puree**
- **5 ounces hot water**
- **1 large onion, diced**
- **1 medium green pepper, diced**

1 teaspoon salt
¼ teaspoon pepper
2 cups uncooked rice

Sauté onion and green pepper in 1 teaspoon margarine until transparent. Add tomatoes, water, salt, and pepper, cooking until hot. Spray large casserole dish with cooking spray. Pour hot liquid and 2 cups raw rice into casserole. Mix well. Bake covered in a 400-degree oven for 1½ hours.

I think my sister Bev gave me the following recipe and I have used it many times while living in Maine. If you haven't ever eaten Maine shrimp, you are in for a treat. Maine shrimp are small and sweet. The going price for five pounds of Maine shrimp was $1 when I was first married. My father would buy shrimp by the bushel. My mother, sister, and I had to clean and behead them. Then they were bagged and frozen to eat all year long. They are caught mainly in December and January.

Maine Shrimp Casserole

1½ cups crushed bacon-flavored crackers
⅔ cup margarine or butter
1 or 2 tablespoons dried chives
¼ teaspoon garlic powder
Approximately 3 to 4 cups uncooked shelled Maine shrimp

Melt margarine or butter with spices. Coat shrimp with butter mixture, then coat with crumbs. Place in a buttered, shallow casserole dish and bake for 20 minutes at 350 degrees.

I developed the following recipe for haddock roll-ups according to our taste. Make sure not to overcook. Cook only until haddock flakes. In Maine, Icelandic haddock used to be plentiful and fairly economical. It is a wonderful tasting fish, without the fishy smell. I used to buy it in a five-pound box, which I believe had been frozen on the boat.

Haddock Roll-ups

1½ to 2 pounds haddock fillets
6 tablespoons margarine or butter, melted
approximately ⅔ cup imitation crab, chopped
3 slices day-old bread, crumbled
1 to 2 tablespoons thinly diced celery
salt and pepper
paprika
parsley flakes
1 cup shredded cheese of choice

Lightly sauté chopped celery in margarine in microwave oven. Add chopped imitation crab, breadcrumbs, salt, pepper, parsley, paprika, and cheese until well mixed. The mixture should be moist.

Place approximately ⅓ to ½ cup stuffing mixture on one end of rinsed and wiped dry fish fillet and roll up. Continue until fillets and stuffing mixture are used up. Place each rolled fillet seam-side down in a greased baking dish. Sprinkle tops with salt, pepper, paprika, and parsley flakes. Bake in a 350-degree oven for approximately 20 to 30 minutes or until fish flakes. Be careful not to overbake!

Chicken or Steak Lo Mein

1 pound London Broil steak or 1 pound boneless, skinless chicken breasts cut into thin strips against the grain
1 teaspoon beef or chicken bouillon
¾ cup water
¼ cup soy sauce
2 tablespoons cornstarch
2 tablespoons cooking oil
1 garlic clove, minced
2 cups shredded cabbage
1 cup diagonally sliced carrots, partially cooked
1 medium onion, chopped
½ cup sliced fresh mushrooms
½ cup finely chopped celery
⅓ cup sliced green onions
15 fresh snow pea pods or 1 package of frozen
This is why I grow and freeze snow pea pods.
1-8-ounce can sliced water chestnuts, drained
4 ounces thin spaghetti, cooked and drained

Combine bouillon, water, soy sauce, and cornstarch; set aside. In wok or large skillet, heat oil on medium-high. Add meat and garlic; stir-fry until the meat is no longer pink, about 5 minutes. Remove meat to a platter. Add cabbage, carrots, onion, mushrooms, celery, and green onions; stir-fry for about 3 minutes. Add pea pods and water chestnuts; stir-fry 2 minutes. Add meat. Stir bouillon mixture and pour into skillet; cook and stir until thickened. Gently toss in spaghetti and heat through for 1 minute. Makes 6 servings.

We rarely ate pork, but when we did, the following recipe was my favorite. The tangy sauce is very good.

Roast Pork with Tangy Sauce

½ teaspoon each salt and garlic salt
2½ teaspoons chili powder, divided
1 rolled and tied boneless pork top loin roast (about 4 pounds)
2 tablespoons vinegar
1 cup apple jelly
1 cup ketchup

In a small bowl combine salt, garlic salt, and ½ teaspoon chili powder; rub on roast. Place roast, fat side up, on rack in shallow roasting pan. Roast in preheated 325-degree oven about 2 hours, or until meat thermometer inserted in center registers 170 degrees. Meanwhile in medium saucepan, combine jelly, ketchup, vinegar, and remaining 2 teaspoons chili powder. Bring to a boil; reduce heat and simmer, uncovered, 2 minutes; set aside. Approximately 15 minutes before roast is done, brush with some jelly mixture. When roast is done, remove from oven and let stand 10 minutes before carving. Mix ½ cup pan drippings with remaining jelly mixture. Reheat sauce, if necessary, and serve with roast. Makes 12 servings.

Surprise Chicken

2 cut-up chickens
1 8-ounce bottle French dressing
1 envelope onion soup mix
1 small can jellied cranberry sauce

Mix all together, except chicken, and pour over chicken that has been placed in a greased baking dish with high sides. Cook uncovered for 50 to 60 minutes at 400 degrees, or until chicken juices run clear.

The following recipe is my favorite crispy-fried chicken recipe; however, I have not made this in a very long time due to the fat content.

Crispy-Fried Chicken

2½ to 3 pounds cut-up frying chicken, or chicken parts
oil for deep-frying
Seasoned Flour:
1½ cups all-purpose flour
1 tablespoon garlic salt
¼ teaspoon poultry seasoning
1½ teaspoons black pepper
1½ teaspoons paprika
Combine all ingredients and set aside.
Crispy Batter:
⅔ cup all-purpose flour
1 beaten egg yolk
¾ cup water
⅛ teaspoon pepper
½ teaspoon salt

Combine flour and seasonings in medium bowl. Combine egg yolk and water. Add gradually to dry ingredients. Heat cooking oil to 365 degrees in deep saucepan or deep fryer to a depth of about 2 inches. Moisten chicken pieces. Dip in seasoned flour, then batter, and then back in seasoned flour. Fry in hot oil for 15 to 18 minutes, or until well browned. Drain on paper. Makes 4 servings.

My sons really like this lemon chicken recipe. The chicken is very moist. I used to make it in an electric frying pan; however, a large skillet would work just as well.

Lemon Chicken

⅓ cup flour
1 teaspoon salt
1 chicken bouillon cube
1 teaspoon paprika
1 frying chicken (2½ to 3 pounds), cut up
3 tablespoons lemon juice
3 tablespoons cooking oil
1½ teaspoons grated lemon peel
¼ cup sliced green onion
2 tablespoons brown sugar

In a paper bag, combine flour, salt, and paprika. Brush chicken with lemon juice. Add 2 pieces of chicken at a time to bag and shake well. In large skillet, brown chicken in hot oil (325 degrees). Dissolve bouillon cube in ¾ cup boiling water; pour over chicken. Stir in onion, brown sugar, peel, and any remaining lemon juice. Cover; reduce heat. Cook chicken over low heat until tender, 40 to 45 minutes. Makes 4 servings.

Aloha Pork

1 pound lean boneless pork shoulder
1 egg
⅓ cup all-purpose flour
½ teaspoon salt
2 tablespoons water
1-20-ounce can pineapple chunks in juice
1 tablespoon sugar
1 tablespoon cornstarch
¼ cup salad oil
2 tablespoons vinegar
2 tablespoons soy sauce
3 medium-sized carrots, pared and sliced thin diagonally
1 large green pepper, halved, seeded, and cut into strips

Cut pork into 1-inch cubes. Beat egg with flour, salt, and water until smooth in a medium-sized bowl; stir in pork cubes until evenly coated. Drain juice from pineapple into a small bowl. Mix sugar and cornstarch in a small bowl; stir in vinegar, soy sauce, and pineapple juice. Heat 3 tablespoons of the salad oil in a large skillet or Dutch oven; add pork cubes and stir-fry 10 minutes, or until meat is browned and tender; remove from skillet with a slotted spoon and drain on paper toweling. Add remaining 1 tablespoon salad oil to skillet; stir in carrots; cook 2 minutes. Stir in green pepper strips; cook 2 minutes, or just until vegetables are crisp-tender. Stir in cornstarch mixture; stir constantly and cook slowly until sauce thickens and boils 1 minute. Stir in pork and pineapple chunks; heat until bubbly. Spoon onto a deep serving platter. Serve with cooked white rice. Makes 6 servings.

The following is an old recipe. I think this was served in the school lunch program when I was in elementary school. They're sort of like Sloppy Joes, but without the tomato base.

Scrambled Hamburger

2 pounds hamburger
1 teaspoon grated onion
1 teaspoon seasoned salt
1 can condensed chicken gumbo soup

Brown hamburger in skillet; drain. Add remaining ingredients and let simmer 10 to 15 minutes. Serve on toasted hamburger rolls.

Salmon Loaf

2 eggs
3 slices soft bread, cubed
¼ cup butter or margarine, melted
1 large can red or pink salmon
1 teaspoon salt
1½ cups milk

Break eggs into bowl and beat until light. Drain salmon; remove skin and bones and flake. Add to eggs, with bread, salt, and butter. Heat milk to lukewarm then add to first mixture. Mix thoroughly. Place in greased loaf pan. Bake in oven at 350 degrees for 1 hour. Makes 6 servings. I think this recipe might be older than I am!

This lazy man's meat loaf is one I have made many times during our busy years. I used to buy ground round in ten-pound packages, which I froze in two to five-pound packages. In the morning I would spray the inside of a slow cooker with nonstick spray, place the block of frozen hamburger in the cooker, and pour a can of undiluted soup over the meat and cook on low all day. Often, I used beef broth or cream of mushroom soup. Steve's mother gave me the recipe that I'm sure she developed.

Lazy Man's Meat Loaf

2 pounds frozen hamburger
1 can undiluted soup of choice or 1 beef bouillon
cube dissolved in 1 cup hot water, cooled

Spray slow cooker with nonstick spray. Place meat in cooker and pour soup over meat. Turn slow cooker on low and cook all day. Season as desired.

Mushroom Meat Loaf

1-3-ounce can mushrooms
milk
1 egg
1 teaspoon salt
1½ pounds ground beef
1½ teaspoons Worcestershire sauce
½ teaspoon dry mustard
dash of pepper
1½ cups soft breadcrumbs

Mix all ingredients together with just enough milk to keep

moist. Place in greased loaf pan. Bake for 1 hour at 350 degrees. Mix 2 tablespoons ketchup and 1 tablespoon light corn syrup and brush on loaf. Bake 15 minutes more. I like to bake some potatoes at the same time to go with the meal.

Sweet and Sour Chicken #1

1-8-ounce bottle Russian dressing
1 package dry onion soup mix
1-12-ounce jar apricot preserves

Mix 3 ingredients together and pour over cut-up chicken parts in greased baking pan. Cook for 1½ hours at 350 degrees, turning once, cooking until tender.

The following sweet and sour recipe is one that I used to make while living in Honduras. I could make it in the cool morning and put it in the Crock-Pot on low. It was a good company meal, especially if I wasn't sure what time company would be there. Pineapple was inexpensive and plentiful. The recipe calls for cut-up, cooked chicken, which was a great way to use up leftover baked chicken. Buy a six or seven-pound roasting chicken or two small chickens and you will have enough leftover to make this recipe.

Sweet and Sour Chicken #2

4 cups cooked, boneless cut-up chicken
1 cup water
6 tablespoons cornstarch
1½ cups brown sugar
2 teaspoons salt

1 large can pineapple chunks (2 cups fresh), reserving canned juice or pureeing some fresh
½ cup white vinegar
4 tablespoons soy sauce
1 small jar maraschino cherries, halved
1 medium onion, cut up
1 medium green pepper, chunked

In a saucepan, combine 1 cup water, cornstarch, brown sugar, and salt. Stir until mixture is smooth. Add reserved pineapple juice or same amount of fresh pureed pineapple. Cook over medium heat 5 to 7 minutes until mixture starts to thicken. Add chicken, soy sauce, and vinegar. Cover and simmer 15 minutes, stirring occasionally. Spray skillet with vegetable cooking spray and sauté onion and green peppers until crisp-tender. Add pineapple chunks, onion, green peppers, and cherry halves to the chicken mixture. Cook until heated or place in Crock-Pot on low. Serve over hot cooked rice. Makes a large amount.

Italian Baked Stuffed Shells

Cheese Filling:
32 ounces ricotta cheese
¼ cup grated Romano cheese
½ teaspoon pepper
1 tablespoon chopped parsley
8 ounces mozzarella cheese, shredded
2 eggs
½ teaspoon salt
¼ cup grated parmesan cheese

Combine all ingredients in a large bowl. Mix by hand with a

wooden spoon or wire whisk until smooth. Place cheese filling in the refrigerator to chill while making meat sauce.

Italian Meat Sauce:

⅓ cup olive oil
1 pound lean hamburger
1 cup diced onion
1 tablespoon Italian seasoning
1½ tablespoons garlic, minced
1 teaspoon black pepper
1 pound Italian sausage, sliced
1 teaspoon salt
1-48-ounce jar spaghetti sauce

Put olive oil in large preheated pot, then add onions and garlic. Sauté 5 minutes or until transparent, being careful not to burn. Add Italian sausage and hamburger; cook about 8 minutes or until fully cooked. Add Italian seasoning, salt, and pepper to pot. Cook and stir well. Stir in spaghetti sauce. Simmer sauce for 15 to 20 minutes and remove from heat.

Final Preparation:

Prepare shells as directed on package. Put ⅓ cheese mixture in a 2-quart plastic bag, cut the corner off the bag and squeeze cheese filling into shell. Repeat until all shells and cheese mixture have been used.

Spray glass 9"x 13" pan with nonstick cooking spray. Put 1½ cups sauce in baking dish, and smooth out evenly. Place shells on sauce, cheese side down. Pour remaining sauce over shells and bake in oven at 350 degrees for 45 minutes. Remove from oven and serve.

Sweet and Sour Meatballs

⅔ cups evaporated milk
½ cups chopped onion
¼ cup brown sugar
1 teaspoon salt
⅔ cups quick oatmeal
¼ cup vinegar
2 tablespoons soy sauce
1½ pounds hamburger
2 tablespoons flour
1-20-ounce can pineapple chunks
1 cup coarsely chopped green pepper

Mix milk, onion, salt, oatmeal, and hamburger in bowl; form into balls the size of walnuts. Brown in skillet. Drain pineapple; reserve juice. Combine juice with enough water to make 1 cup; add flour, brown sugar, vinegar, and soy sauce. Heat until thickened and clear. Add pineapple and peppers. Place meatballs in casserole dish. Pour sauce over meatballs. Bake about 30 minutes at 350 degrees. Makes 10 to 12 servings.

Chinese Egg Rolls

1-pound can bean sprouts
1 can shrimp (fresh Maine shrimp are best)
½ teaspoon sugar
½ pound ground pork or hamburger
1 tablespoon soy sauce
1 tablespoon cornstarch
2 teaspoons salt
3 tablespoons cooking oil
2 cups chopped celery, including leaves

2 cups regular or Chinese cabbage, shredded
1 package egg roll wrappers (found in the produce
department of your supermarket)

Rinse bean sprouts and set aside.

Set wok on high heat. Pour in 1 tablespoon oil and swirl over high heat until it is very hot. Add meat and stir-fry until it loses its reddish color, then add the soy sauce and sugar. Stir-fry for another minute. Remove from wok and set aside. Pour in remaining 2 tablespoons oil and add celery and cabbage; stir-fry for 5 minutes or until soft. Add the salt and bean sprouts and stir until combined. Cook until liquid begins to boil. There should be 2 to 3 tablespoons of liquid in wok; if there is more, discard.

Stir cornstarch into liquid until thick and mix with mixture. Add shrimp. Cool.

Place egg roll wrapper so it is diamond shaped. Put approximately ⅓ cup of filling in middle of wrapper. Wet upper two edges of wrapper with water, bring lowest corner up over filling, then fold over right side and left side. Finally, bring down top corner. Make sure all edges are secured. Wet with more water if necessary. Deep fry in hot oil until wrapper is golden brown.

To lower the fat content, use nonstick spray to coat the tops of the egg rolls. Place on a baking sheet that's also sprayed with nonstick cooking spray and bake in a preheated 425-degree oven for 10 to 15 minutes. Sometimes I substitute preshredded coleslaw mix for the cabbage. The addition of the carrots that are in the coleslaw mix makes the egg rolls more colorful and flavorful. Also, since it is preshredded it eliminates one step. Sometimes I need the extra time.

Carolyn's Sweet and Sour Pork

In paper bag combine:

¼ cup flour
1 teaspoon salt
dash black pepper
Add
2 pounds boneless pork cut into 1-inch cubes; shake to coat. In Dutch oven, brown meat in hot oil.
Combine:
1 cup water
½ cup ketchup
½ cup vinegar
1 tablespoon Worcestershire sauce
¼ cup brown sugar
1 teaspoon salt

Stir into meat. Add 1 cup chopped onion. Cover and cook over low heat for 1 hour and 45 minutes, stirring occasionally. Add one 6-ounce package frozen pea pods, partially thawed, and cook 5 minutes more. You can also make this in a slow cooker as my mother-in-law did.

The following is another recipe that was from my deceased mother-in-law. I use this sauce for cooking mini hot dogs and diagonal-sliced kielbasa, as well as meatballs. I almost always use this recipe at Christmastime for entertaining and I think of Carolyn; she loved entertaining.

Carolyn's Sweet and Sour Meatballs

2 pounds hamburger
2 slices bread, made into fine crumbs
½ cup minced onion
½ cup milk, to soften breadcrumbs
1 egg
1 teaspoon salt
1/8 teaspoon pepper

Mix together and form into small balls. Drop uncooked meatballs into following heated sauce.

Sauce:

1-10-ounce jar grape jelly
1-12-ounce bottle ketchup

Let meatballs simmer, uncovered. Serve in a chafing dish or Crock-Pot, keeping them hot and using toothpicks for spearing.

I really like the following Swedish meatball recipe. I think it was from my Aunt Pearl.

Swedish Meatballs

1 pound hamburger
1 cup breadcrumbs
1½ cups cornflakes, slightly crushed

1 onion, chopped
½ cup milk
2 egg yolks, beaten
1 teaspoon salt
3 tablespoons cooking oil
⅛ teaspoon pepper
2 egg whites
1 can cream of mushroom or cream of chicken soup

Combine combine hamburger, breadcrumbs, onion, milk, egg yolk, salt and pepper; mix well. Form into balls. Dip into slightly beaten egg whites and roll in crushed cornflakes. Brown on all sides in hot oil.

Place in a baking dish. Add soup mixed with ½ cup water and pour over meatballs. Bake for 30 minutes in a 350-degree oven. Makes 6 servings.

The following recipe is very economical to make and very tasty. Usually around St. Patrick's Day in March, cabbage is very inexpensive. In my Maine hometown, many older people make this recipe to serve on St. Patrick's Day. My family really enjoyed this casserole.

Corned Beef and Cabbage Casserole

5 medium potatoes, thinly sliced
1 can corned beef
1 small onion, chopped
4 cups shredded cabbage
1 teaspoon salt
1/8 teaspoon pepper
1 can cream of celery soup

1½ cups milk

Place potatoes in greased, shallow 9" x 13" baking pan. Cover with onions, salt, and pepper. Add shredded cabbage, then crumble corned beef on top of that. Cover with celery soup that has been diluted with the milk.

Cover with foil; bake 1½ to 2 hours at 350 degrees. This makes a large casserole.

Curly Noodle Pork Supper

1 pound pork tenderloin, cut into ¼-inch strips. (Chicken can be substituted.)
1 medium sweet red pepper, cut into 1-inch pieces
1 cup broccoli florets
4 green onions, cut into 1-inch pieces
1 tablespoon vegetable oil
1½ cups water
2-3-ounce packages Teriyaki chicken ramen noodles
1 tablespoon minced fresh or dried parsley
1 tablespoon soy sauce

In a large skillet or wok, cook pork, red pepper, broccoli, and onions in oil until meat is no longer pink. Add the water, noodles with contents of seasoning packets, parsley, and soy sauce. Bring to a boil. Reduce heat; cook for 3 to 4 minutes or until noodles are tender. Makes 3 to 4 servings.

Tater Taco Casserole

2 pounds ground beef
¼ cup chopped onion

1 envelope taco seasoning
⅔ cup water
1-11-ounce can whole kernel corn, drained
1-11-ounce can condensed fiesta nacho cheese soup, or 1 can cheddar cheese soup and 1 small can chopped green chilies
1-32-ounce package frozen tater tots

In a skillet, cook beef and onion over medium heat until meat is no longer pink; drain. Stir in taco seasoning and water. Simmer uncovered for 5 minutes. Add corn and soup; mix well.

Transfer to a greased 9" x 13" x 2" baking dish. Arrange tater tots in a single layer over the top. Bake uncovered at 350 degrees for 30 to 35 minutes, or until potatoes are crispy and golden brown. Makes 8 servings.

Years ago a friend made these tuna burger sandwiches for Steve and me when we visited her in Jackman, Maine. I used to make them when I had company coming for lunch. They are very good and would stretch a can of tuna when we were on a tight food budget during Steve's college days.

Tuna Burgers

1 or 2 cans tuna fish
1 can cream of chicken soup

Years ago tuna came in 8-ounce cans, but now that they come in 6-ounce cans I would use two in this recipe. Drain tuna and mix with soup. Blend well. Place part of mixture on a slice of bread. Continue until all is used. Place under broiler for approximately 5 minutes or until bubbly. Remove and place a slice of buttered bread on top of each burger, buttered side up. Place under broiler again until tops are evenly light brown, watching closely.

Fried Chicken Nuggets with Sweet an Sour Sauce

1 chicken, cooked and cut up into chunks, without bone
½ cup all-purpose flour
½ teaspoon salt
½ cup cornstarch
1 egg
1 teaspoon baking powder
1 quart cooking oil
1 teaspoon sugar
sweet and sour sauce (recipe to follow)

Combine the flour, cornstarch, baking powder, sugar, and salt. Combine egg with ⅔ cup ice water in blender. Add dry ingredients, cover and process at medium speed for 1 minute. Pour oil into 5-quart Dutch oven, filling no more than ⅓ full. Heat to 375 degrees over medium heat. Dip chicken pieces in batter, then drain and fry by putting a few pieces in the oil at a time, turning once; fry about 4 minutes, or until crisp and brown.

Serve with sweet and sour sauce. I don't usually think of sweet and sour sauce containing canned tomatoes, but this next sauce recipe includes it and it's delicious!

Sweet and Sour Sauce

1½ cups sugar
1 cup canned tomatoes
1 tablespoon cornstarch
½ cup chopped onion
½ cup cider vinegar
1 tablespoon soy sauce
1 teaspoon ground ginger
¼ teaspoon salt
½ cup crushed pineapple
1 green pepper, cut into 1-inch squares

Combine sugar, tomatoes, pineapple, onion, vinegar, soy sauce, ginger, and salt. Bring to a boil and simmer uncovered for 20 minutes. Blend cornstarch and 2 tablespoons of water to make a smooth paste; add to sauce and heat to boiling. Boil for 1 minute, or until it reaches a smooth consistency. Remove from heat and add green pepper; let stand for 4 minutes. This sauce is very good for dipping chicken pieces.

Chicken Lo Mein

¼ pound fine egg noodles
¼ pound cooked chicken
2½ tablespoons cornstarch
6 mushrooms
2 stalks celery
2½ tablespoons soy sauce
2½ tablespoons cooking oil
¼ cup chicken broth
4 tablespoons water

salt and pepper to taste

Cook the noodles in boiling water. Rinse in cold water and drain. Cut chicken and vegetables into shreds. Sauté chicken in the hot oil for about 2 minutes. Add vegetables and sauté for another 2 minutes. Add chicken broth and mix well. Cover, reduce heat, and simmer for about 10 minutes. Mix together cornstarch, water, and soy sauce and add to the chicken and vegetable mixture. Season to taste with salt and pepper. Stir in the noodles, re-heat, and serve immediately. Makes 4 to 6 servings.

I got the following recipe from one of my hometown cookbooks, *Albion's Country Cooking*. It's very good, quick, and easy to prepare. Cutting up the chicken in bite-sized pieces makes this recipe great for potluck suppers. You should reduce the cooking time if you cut the chicken breasts into small pieces.

Stuffing Good Chicken

8 boneless, skinless chicken breasts, more or less
1-8-ounce package Swiss cheese, shredded or sliced works well
1 can cream of chicken soup
¾ cup chicken broth
½ cup butter, melted
1-8-ounce package Pepperidge Farm stuffing mix

Put chicken in 9" x 13" baking dish. Lay cheese over chicken. Mix soup and chicken broth with wire whisk and pour evenly over chicken and cheese. Dump dry stuffing over all and spread evenly. Pour melted butter over stuffing. Bake at

350 degrees for 45 minutes. (This can be made the night before and baked the next day, 50 minutes if cold from the refrigerator.)

Breakfast Pizza

1 pound sausage
1 cup grated cheddar cheese
2 tablespoons milk
5 eggs
1 package of refrigerated crescent rolls

Brown sausage, crumble, and drain well. Press out rolls on a round pizza pan. Spread sausage, sprinkle cheese, then pour beaten eggs and milk over the top. Bake at 350 degrees for 25 minutes, or until brown. I like crumbled, cooked bacon better than the sausage. I have even used crumbled real bacon from a jar and it works well.

Baked Scallops

Put about 4 tablespoons butter or margarine in a shallow glass baking pan. Preheat oven to 400 degrees. While preheating, put the baking pan in the oven to melt the butter. Watch closely to avoid burning.

Wash and dry scallops. Place Ritz cracker crumbs into a pie plate. Roll the dried scallops in melted butter, then roll in crumbs; place back into the buttered baking dish. Continue until all scallops are prepared, being careful to separate them so they will bake quickly. Salt and pepper scallops. Bake at 400 degrees for 15 to 20 minutes. Don't overcook! Bay scallops are small and cook quickly. Sea scallops are larger and take about 15 to 20 minutes.

The following recipe is the one I started using when I was first married. Many, many meat loafs later, I tend not to measure, but always use the same ingredients.

Meat Loaf

1½ to 2 pounds hamburger
1½ cups breadcrumbs
1 egg, beaten
1½ cups milk
½ teaspoon salt
pinch of poultry seasoning
dash of black pepper
1 tablespoon ketchup
¼ cup finely chopped onion

Mix breadcrumbs, milk, egg, and seasonings together in bowl and allow crumbs to soften for a half hour or so. Then mix in the hamburger so that the dressing is well mixed into the meat. Turn lightly into a greased loaf pan. I spread a thin layer of ketchup on the top of the meat loaf and a few sprinkles of Parmesan cheese. Bake for 1 hour at 400 degrees, 1 ¼ hours at 375 degrees, or for 1 ½ hours at 350 degrees. I usually bake potatoes at the same time.

Porcupine Meat Balls

½ cup raw rice, (not instant) soaked in cold water 1 hour
1 pound hamburger
½ cup breadcrumbs
1 tablespoon minced onion
1 can tomato soup
1 soup can of water
1 teaspoon salt
¼ teaspoon pepper

Soaking the rice ensures that the rice will be cooked when the meatballs are cooked through. Mix all ingredients together, except soup and water. Make into meatballs. Place in covered casserole dish to bake. Mix together tomato soup and water, then pour over meatballs. Bake covered at 375 degrees for 1 hour.

Hotdog Macaroni Casserole

1 can condensed cheddar cheese soup
1 can condensed tomato soup
½ cup water
¼ cup finely minced onion
2 teaspoons prepared mustard
5 cups cooked macaroni
6 to 10 hotdogs

Stir cheese soup, tomato soup, water, onion, and mustard until smooth. Add macaroni. Pour into shallow 7" x 11" baking dish. Arrange hotdogs on top. Bake at 400 degrees for 25 minutes.

Beef and Broccoli

1 pound London broil steak
2 bunches broccoli
1 tablespoon cornstarch or flour in ½ cup water
1 teaspoon sugar and garlic powder
salt and pepper to taste
2 tablespoons cooking oil
2 tablespoons soy sauce

Cut beef against the grain in thin slices; add salt, pepper, sugar, garlic powder, and soy sauce. Let stand 30 minutes in the refrigerator. Cut broccoli into bite-sized pieces. Take off outer rough skin, if you wish. Place 1 tablespoon oil in hot cooking pan. Stir-fry beef, searing quickly until no longer pink. Remove meat from pan. Put the other 1 tablespoon oil in pan and stir-fry broccoli until crisp tender. Add salt, pepper, and water while burner is still on high so that steam can go through broccoli. Thicken with cornstarch and water mixture. Stir in the beef and cook 1 minute. Serve over fluffy white rice. Makes 6 servings.

Taco Pie

1 package taco seasoning mix
1 package crescent dinner rolls
2 cups crushed corn chips
8 oz. fat-free sour cream
1 cup low-fat shredded cheddar cheese
½ cup salsa
1 pound lean ground beef

Brown and drain the ground beef. Add seasoning mix, water

(according to seasoning mix directions), and salsa; simmer 15 minutes. Put rolls in a 9-inch pie plate to form a crust. Layer 1 cup of crushed corn chips, ½ ground beef mixture, ½ of sour cream, cheese, ground beef, sour cream, cheese, and corn chips. Drizzle a little salsa over top, then bake at 350 degrees for 30 minutes. Let stand 10 minutes before slicing and serving.

My family really enjoys homemade lasagna and it's one of those recipes that is great to serve when company is coming. I usually make two at a time, freezing one and keeping the other one for guests. The problem comes when I'm asked for the recipe, because I don't use one. I can list the ingredients and the steps to put it together; however, the measurements are not exact. I use a 9" x 13" and an 11" x 15" glass baking pan. Not too long ago I worked with my daughter Sarah in her kitchen to show her how to make the lasagna. Since I didn't have a recipe to give her, she wrote down the steps as we went.

Jean's Lasagna

I start this recipe, which makes two large lasagnas, by browning 2 to 2 ½ pounds hamburger. When this is done and drained, I sprinkle some garlic powder on the meat. I use 2 large 32-ounce jars of spaghetti sauce (I often use Ragu) and combine with ground beef and add about 2 teaspoons sugar. I either simmer this together on the stove or in the microwave. Often I will cook the ground beef in the microwave. While the sauce is simmering, I mix together 1 egg with a large container of ricotta cheese in a large bowl. I then sprinkle approximately 1 teaspoon parsley flakes over the egg and cheese mixture. I usually buy shredded Mozzarella cheese in 5-pound packages, and always have grated Parmesan cheese on hand. This recipe uses one 1-pound box of lasagna noodles. I do not cook the noodles before assembling the lasagna; by doing this it saves time and avoids another pot to wash. Because you aren't cooking the noodles, it's best to make this one day ahead of when you will be serving it. I like this recipe because it isn't as liquid as some lasagnas tend to be. The noodles absorb some of the sauce. Freezing the second casserole right away after assembling works well.

Assembling:

Spray both baking pans with nonstick cooking spray. Using a soup ladle, spread some sauce evenly over the bottom of each pan, not too thin since you need the liquid in the sauce to soften the noodles. On top of the noodles add another layer of sauce, a layer of ricotta cheese, then a good layer of Mozzarella cheese. Sprinkle with Parmesan cheese. Add one more layer of noodles, then sauce, followed by ricotta, mozzarella, and Parmesan. Spray one side of a sheet of heavy-duty aluminum foil with nonstick cooking spray and place over the top of each baking pan, folding the edges snugly around the pan. The nonstick cooking spray will prevent the cheese from sticking to the aluminum foil. Freeze one pan and place the other in the refrigerator to cook the next day. You might not need all of the sauce. You have to use enough, but not an excessive amount. I bake the lasagna at 375 to 400 degrees uncovered for about 45 minutes or however long it takes to become bubbly around the edges and when a knife inserted in the center comes out hot. If it's not brown on the top but tests done, place the pan under the broiler for a few minutes, watching closely to make sure it doesn't become too brown. Let set for about 10 minutes before serving. Enjoy!

Vegetables

Slow-Cooked Broccoli

2-10-ounce packages frozen chopped broccoli, partially thawed
1 can condensed cream of celery soup, undiluted
1½ cups shredded sharp cheddar cheese, divided
¼ cup chopped onion or dried onion equivalent
½ teaspoon Worcestershire sauce
¼ teaspoon pepper
approximately 25 butter-flavored crackers, crushed
2 tablespoons butter or margarine, melted

In greased slow cooker, combine broccoli, soup, 1 cup cheese, onion, Worcestershire sauce, and pepper. Combine cracker crumbs with melted butter and sprinkle over top. Cover and cook on high for about 2 hours. Sprinkle remaining ½ cup of shredded cheese over top and cook 10 minutes longer. Makes 8 to 10 servings. I have tried substituting cream of chicken soup and Swiss cheese, but we did not care for the flavor as well.

Candied Sweet Potatoes

1 cup dark corn syrup
½ cup firmly packed dark brown sugar
2 tablespoons butter or margarine
12 medium cooked sweet potatoes, peeled, and halved lengthwise

Bring first 3 ingredients to boil. Reduce heat; simmer 5 minutes. Pour half into large shallow baking dish. Add potatoes and top with remaining syrup. Bake in 350-degree oven, basting often, for 20 minutes. Makes 12 servings.

The following recipe tastes just as good reheated, which allows you to make it a day ahead. I like to make this as a side dish for Easter dinner. Making it ahead cuts down on the cooking I have to do on Easter Sunday, when I am always so pressed for time.

Sweet Potato Casserole

3 cups mashed sweet potatoes
¾ cup sugar
½ teaspoon salt
2 eggs, beaten
½ cup milk
1 teaspoon vanilla

Combine above ingredients and place in shallow baking dish. In a separate bowl mix:

1 cup brown sugar
1 cup chopped pecans (optional)
½ cup flour
4 tablespoons butter or margarine, melted

Mix until crumbly with a pastry blender; add this to the top of the sweet potatoes. Bake at 400 degrees for 35 minutes.

Sweet Potato Pie

3 medium sweet potatoes, boiled and mashed
1 stick butter
1 cup white sugar
1-5-ounce can evaporated milk
½ cup milk
4 eggs, beaten
½ teaspoon vanilla

Beat potatoes and butter until smooth. Add sugar and eggs. Beat well. Add milk and vanilla. Pour into an unbaked pie shell. Bake for 30 minutes at 350 degrees.

I came across this spicy home-fried potato recipe by accident; it was a recipe within another recipe that my family really did not care for. This recipe makes a large batch of home fries, which makes it a great company recipe. Since I have a recipe for Italian salad dressing mix, I usually don't buy the mix that this calls for. I took these home fries to a luncheon at a Bible study in Honduras and was feeling guilty because they didn't look so great, but to my surprise they were a big hit.

Spicy Home Fries

4½ pounds potatoes, peeled and cut into ¾-inch chunks
¼ cup olive or vegetable oil
2-7-ounce envelopes Italian salad dressing mix

In a large bowl, toss the potatoes with oil and dressing mixes or put all ingredients in a large clean plastic zipper bag and shake well. Place into two greased 9" x 13" baking pans. Bake in a 400-degree oven for 45 minutes, or until tender.

My friend Kiyoko, who is Japanese, always liked to serve fresh cucumbers this way.

Kiyoko's Cucumbers

Slice thin a peeled cucumber, then sprinkle with salt. Mix together using your hands. Rinse cucumbers, then squeeze to get rid of the excess water. In another bowl, mix together a little vinegar, sugar, and soy sauce, using more soy sauce than vinegar. Add drained cucumbers. Let cucumbers marinate for at least 30 minutes.

Bean sprouts are nice to have on a salad or in a sandwich. They are a good source of vitamins, very easy to grow yourself, and much cheaper than buying them. I used to grow these quite often; however, several years ago I read that you can get food poisoning from some types of sprouts and I don't see people using them as often. I stored mine in the refrigerator and if they started to look wilted or were more than a week old, I discarded them. I found that a small amount of alfalfa seeds are inexpensive to buy in a health food store, take up very little storage space, and keep well in the freezer. I came across these instructions to grow bean sprouts back in 1985, and have grown them many times. Make sure you follow the instructions carefully so you grow a safe product.

Bean Sprouts

Use a quart-size, wide-mouth, clear canning jar or a quart-size mayonnaise jar. This type of jar allows you to watch the growth process and it holds enough sprouts to serve 4 to 6 people.

Cut a 6" x 6" square of fine nylon mesh material, stretch it over the jar and hold with a heavy rubber band. Do not use cheesecloth because it can get soggy. The key to growing your own sprouts is to keep the seeds moist, enable air to circulate, and to keep the temperature warm. I prefer alfalfa seeds, however I have also tried broccoli seeds. Only use seeds that are meant to be used for sprouts. I recommend buying them at a health food store, seeds meant to grow in a garden are, as I understand it, chemically treated.

Starting by placing 2 teaspoons or up to 1 tablespoon of alfalfa seeds into the clean jar, covering with enough warm water to be about ½ inch over the seeds. Place the nylon mesh fabric over the jar, securing tightly with a rubber band. Soak seeds overnight. Next morning, drain off the water through the cover. Run tepid water from the faucet through the mesh, rinse the beans, and drain the water off again.

Set the jar of damp seeds in a dimly lit corner of your kitchen (out of direct sunlight), where temperatures stay around 68 to 70 degrees. This will start the germination process. Lay the jar on its side to expose as many seeds as possible to the air.

Once the seeds are moistened, they must be kept wet by running water into the jar and draining it off several times a day. I do this four times a day, at mealtimes and then at bedtime.

In 2 or 3 days, shoots will appear. Keep on wetting and draining the seeds until the sprouts get to the length you desire. If you want green sprouts instead of white, place the ready-to-harvest seed in a sunny window. If you do not like the seed shells on the sprouts, they can be easily removed by placing the sprouts in a bowl of water and stirring them to loosen the shells. The seeds will float to the top and then you can skim them off.

Grow alfalfa seeds about 1 inch long. Wash the jar and screen in hot soapy water after you are finished growing sprouts, then sterilize the jar and screen in scalding water. Sprouts store well for about a week in a plastic bag in the refrigerator. This process sounds time consuming, but after doing it once it will seem easy.

Broccoli and Cauliflower Bake

2 cups broccoli florets
2 cups cauliflower, cut up
1 can cream of mushroom soup
½ soup can of milk
½ to 1 teaspoon garlic powder
salt and pepper to taste
mozzarella or Swiss cheese, shredded

Partially cook broccoli and cauliflower. Drain and place in a covered casserole dish. Mix together soup, milk, and garlic powder, pour over vegetables. Top with shredded cheese. Bake for 25 minutes in a 325-degree oven.

Oven-Baked Potato Wedges

vegetable cooking spray
4 tablespoons butter or margarine (½ stick)
4 large potatoes (about 2 pounds)

¾ teaspoon black pepper
seasoned salt

About 40 minutes before serving, preheat oven to 425 degrees. Spray 9" x 13" baking pan with vegetable cooking spray; add butter or margarine. Place the pan in the oven to melt butter. Remove pan from oven before butter starts to burn.

Cut washed, unpeeled potatoes lengthwise into 8 wedges. Add potatoes to melted butter in baking pan; sprinkle with pepper and seasoned salt; gently toss to coat. Bake 30 minutes, or until potatoes are tender and evenly browned, turning occasionally.

Instead of using butter or margarine, you can spray potato wedges with vegetable cooking spray for less fat and calories. Often I will substitute extra virgin olive oil for the butter, only using enough olive oil to coat lightly. I usually cook them on a baking pan that is larger than a 9" X 13" pan and the potatoes brown better.

I have used the following corn pudding recipe many times. Not only is it easy and economical, but it cooks so quickly that it's a great last-minute recipe for entertaining!

Microwave Corn Pudding

1 egg
¾ cup crushed crackers, Ritz or Saltines
½ cup milk
2 tablespoons margarine, cut into pieces
1 tablespoon sugar
paprika
1-16-ounce can cream style corn

Place egg in 1½-quart casserole dish and beat well with fork. Stir in milk, sugar, corn, crackers, and butter. Microwave at medium high for 7 minutes and stir well. Sprinkle with paprika. Microwave for 2 minutes more until barely set. Microwave temperatures vary, so watch closely. You may find that you have to adjust this recipe after making it for the first time. Makes about 4 servings. Very easy, quick, and economical!

Microwave Rice Pilaf

1 medium onion, coarsely chopped (½ cup)
1 large celery rib, coarsely chopped (½ cup)
1½ tablespoons margarine
4 ounces medium-sized fresh mushrooms (about 2 cups)
1¾ cups chicken broth
1 cup raw long-grain white rice
1 tablespoon chopped parsley

In a deep, 2-quart casserole dish, microwave onion, celery, and butter on high 2 to 4 minutes until vegetables are crisp-tender. Stir in mushrooms, broth, and rice. Cover with lid or vented plastic wrap. Microwave on high 4 to 6 minutes until boiling. Reduce power to medium. Microwave 15 to 25 minutes until liquid is absorbed. Carefully remove lid; stir in parsley then cover. Let stand for 5 minutes.

A few years ago I found a great deal on a 24-ounce bag of French's onion rings at a shopping club. Since the bag was only $.87, I bought two, one for our pastor's wife and one for me. They freeze well. I did not always have these on hand unless for a holiday meal or if I found a great sale.

Everyday Easy Broccoli Bake

1 can cream of broccoli soup
dash of black pepper
½ cup milk
1 bunch (1½ pound) cooked broccoli, cut up
1 teaspoon soy sauce
1 can French fried onion rings

In a 1½-quart casserole dish combine soup, milk, soy sauce, and pepper. Stir in broccoli and ½ can of the onions. Bake at 350 degrees for 25 minutes or until hot, stir. Top with remaining onions. Bake 5 minutes more.

Or, to microwave: Cook on high 8 minutes covered with wax paper. Top with onions and microwave, uncovered for 1 more minute. Makes 6 servings.

Easy White Rice

I have learned an easy way to cook rice for up to 6 people. Use a large heavy saucepan. Add 1 fistful of white rice (not minute rice) for each serving and one extra for the pot. Add cold water to about 1 inch above rice. You can use your index finger to touch the top of the rice; the water should reach the first bend of your index finger. Place the saucepan over a red-hot burner (if electric) or high flame if gas. Stir rice to prevent sticking, turn heat very low, cover tightly, and simmer for 20 minutes—if using an electric stove, turn off power completely and let simmer on burner for 20 minutes. Do not uncover pot for this cooking period. I find this method easy and reliable!

Breads, Rolls, and Muffins

Baked Oatmeal

3 cups oatmeal
2 cups milk
¾ cup brown sugar
2 teaspoons baking powder
½ cup margarine
1 teaspoon salt
2 eggs

Mix all ingredients together and pour into 9" x 13" buttered pan. Bake at 375 degrees for 25 minutes. I pour milk on a bowl of this as I would a plain bowl of hot oatmeal.

Microwave Quick Oatmeal—1 serving

⅔ cup water
dash of salt
⅓ cup quick oats

Place ingredients in a 2-cup cereal bowl. Microwave on high for 1½ to 2 minutes. This is a recipe from the Quaker Oats container, which I have used for years. Make sure you use at least a 2-cup bowl or it will run over during cooking.

Microwave Old-Fashioned Oatmeal

1 serving

> **1 cup water**
> **dash of salt**
> **½ cup old-fashioned oatmeal**

Place ingredients in a 2-cup or larger bowl and microwave on medium-high for 3 minutes.

The following is a buttermilk pancake recipe that is truly my favorite of any pancake recipes that I have found. They are nice and light and my guests have enjoyed them also. Add 2 cups of Maine blueberries and I would say they are the perfect pancakes!

Buttermilk Pancakes

> **2 eggs, slightly beaten**
> **3 tablespoons sugar**
> **2 cups buttermilk**
> **1 teaspoon salt**
> **2 cups unbleached flour**
> **1 ½ teaspoons baking powder**
> **1 teaspoon baking soda**
> **3 tablespoons vegetable oil**

Using one bowl, beat eggs and then add buttermilk. Add

flour, sugar, salt, and baking powder. Stir. Fold in oil, being careful not to over stir, lumps are okay. Lightly coat griddle with cooking spray. Spoon 4-inch circles of batter onto griddle and turn when puffed up and full of bubbles. Makes 12 to 15 small pancakes. When I use an electric griddle I turn it to 300 degrees.

The following is my favorite tea bread recipe to serve at a party. It's inexpensive and easy.

Lemon Bread

1 cup sugar
1½ cups flour
½ cup shortening
1 teaspoon baking powder
2 eggs
½ teaspoon salt
½ cup milk
grated rind of 1 lemon

Cream sugar and shortening. Beat eggs and add, alternating with milk and rind. Pour in greased loaf pan. Bake at 350 degrees for 55 minutes or until toothpick comes out clean.

Mix:

¼ cup white sugar
juice of one lemon

Pour over loaf when it comes from the oven. Let stand for 10 minutes, then remove from the pan. Makes one 5"x 9" pan of bread.

Pumpkin Bread

4 eggs
2 teaspoons baking soda
⅔ cup water
1½ teaspoons salt
1 cup vegetable oil
1 teaspoon cinnamon
1-16-ounce can pumpkin
1 teaspoon nutmeg
3 ½ cups flour
pinch of cloves
3 cups sugar

Beat eggs; add oil, water, and pumpkin. Mix well with wire whisk. Add dry ingredients, mixing only until moist. If you overmix quick breads or muffins, they will be tough. Bake in a 350-degree oven for 1 hour. Makes 2 loaves.

I use this recipe often to make jumbo pumpkin muffins. The recipe makes 12 jumbo or 24 regular muffins. Sprinkle with coarse sanding sugar before baking for a nice touch. The muffins are done when a toothpick inserted in the center of the muffins comes out clean. If you overbake, the muffins will be dry.

My good friend Nancy Wemhoener gave me her favorite recipe for Focaccia bread, which she has made many times and I have enjoyed because of her generosity. She is a great cook!

Focaccia

1 cup warm water
1 package instant-rise yeast
1 teaspoon sugar
1 tablespoon honey
1¼ teaspoon salt
2 tablespoons extra-virgin olive oil
2 tablespoons semolina flour
1 teaspoon Lawry's Pinch of Herbs Seasoning (Or Nancy's friend that gave her the recipe said that you could use 1–2 tsps. crumbled dried herbs such as rosemary, basil, oregano, or thyme, any or all. Also, she said that you could omit the herbs in the dough and sprinkle them on top of the dough prior to baking.)
1 cup all-purpose flour
1¾ cups bread flour
olive oil for drizzling
kosher or sea salt and freshly ground coarse black pepper to taste
crumbled, dried rosemary (or could use the Tuscan Herbs mill)
shavings of fresh garlic and /or sautéed fresh onion slices

Toppings:

black olives, Tuscany herbs, rosemary, garlic, pepper, Parmesan cheese, and olive oil

In a bowl, whisk the water, yeast, and sugar together. Let stand for 2 to 3 minutes to dissolve the yeast. Stir in the oil and honey; mix. In a food processor, mix the semolina, the all-purpose flour, salt, and 1 cup of the bread flour. Mix until combined. Gradually add more bread flour as needed to form soft, elastic dough. Turn the dough out onto a lightly floured surface and form into a ball. Place the dough in a lightly greased bowl; cover with a tea towel. Let rise for 45 minutes, or until almost doubled.

Deflate the dough and let it rest, covered, 15 minutes longer, or you can also refrigerate the dough in an oiled plastic bag for up to 2 days. Before using, let the dough come to room temperature for about 30 minutes.

Preheat the oven to 425 degrees. Lightly coat a baking sheet or a 15-inch pizza pan with olive oil; wipe out excess. Dust lightly with semolina or cornmeal; knock out any excess. Turn the dough out onto the prepared pan and flatten gently into a round to fit an 11½-inch deep-dish stoneware pizza dish. If the dough resists, or otherwise retracts, let it rest for a few more minutes. Dimple the top of the dough with your fingertips or handle of a wooden spoon. Drizzle with olive oil, and sprinkle with salt, coarse pepper, garlic shavings, onions, and rosemary or Tuscan herbs. Let the focaccia rise in the pan for 45 minutes. Bake for 12 to 14 minutes, or until lightly browned on top. Transfer to a wire rack to cool.

After baking, the bread will be about ¾ inch high. Slice, cut into wedges, or tear off pieces. Serve with olive oil and freshly ground black pepper.

The following is also an old tried-and-true recipe from my old friend Sue Burrill. Since I have been using my bread machine to mix the dough, I use the 2 pound bread dough recipe that came with it. However, this is also a good recipe.

Pizza Dough

1 cup warm water, dissolve 1 package yeast, then add 1 teaspoon sugar, 1 teaspoon salt, 2 tablespoons cooking oil. Add 2 cups flour—more if needed.

Knead—let rise till double in bulk. Split in half for pans or use whole thing on a cookie sheet. Bake pizza in a 425-degree oven until done.

Bread Machine Pizza Dough

1½ cups water
2 tablespoons olive oil
2 tablespoons sugar
1¾ teaspoons salt
4 cups bread flour
2 tablespoons dry milk powder
2½ teaspoons instant active dry yeast

This is for a 2-pound loaf of bread dough. If using your bread machine, place ingredients in container as the machine instructions direct. Most large pizza pans hold about 1 1b. of bread dough. Make sure to spray your pizza pan with nonstick spray. You can brush your dough with olive oil before adding pizza sauce and toppings.

If I am making pizza for just my husband and myself, I divide the dough in half and place half the dough in a quart zip top freezer bag and throw in the freezer for another time. To thaw, I just put the bag in the refrigerator in the morning and by the time I need it for dinner it's thawed. I just tear the bag down the side and plop the dough onto my floured breadboard.

The following is my favorite roll dough. It is so easy with no kneading and you can have fresh rolls every night by making only the number you need for that meal!

Refrigerator Rolls

2 cups lukewarm water
½ cup white sugar
1 ½ teaspoons salt
Mix together, then add:
2 packages yeast or 2 teaspoons bulk yeast
Stir until dissolved. Add:
1 egg
¼ cup soft shortening
Mix in first with wooden spoon, then with hand:
6 to 7 cups sifted flour

Grease top of dough well and place in refrigerator immediately after mixing. Cover with waxed paper or refrigerator cover and then with a damp cloth. About two hours before baking, shape dough into desired number of rolls. Cover and let rise until light. Dough made with water keeps about 5 days in the refrigerator. Punch down occasionally. No kneading! Bake at 400 degrees for 12 to 15 minutes. This makes about 3 dozen rolls.

This next recipe is one given to me by a nurse coworker in the first year that I was married. I have used it regularly ever since. It's a great basic muffin recipe that doubles well. Add whatever fruit you want, such as blueberries, dates, pineapple, etc.

Marge's Muffins

2 cups flour
½ cup white sugar
5 teaspoons baking powder
1 egg
¼ cup cooking oil
1 cup milk
1 cup or more of blueberries, dates, or your choice of fruit

Mix liquids together first then add dry ingredients, adding fruit to flour. Blend together only until well mixed. Fill greased muffin cups about 2/3 full. Bake at 400 degrees for approximately 20 to 25 minutes. Makes 1 dozen muffins.

For a quick and easy batter muffin to use for strawberry shortcake, you can't go wrong with this recipe.

Shortcake Muffins

1½ cups flour
1 tablespoon baking powder
½ teaspoon salt
2 to 4 tablespoons white sugar
¼ cup cold butter or margarine
1 egg
½ cup milk

In a bowl, combine flour, baking powder, salt, and sugar. I like my shortcake sweet, so I use 4 tablespoons sugar instead of 2. Cut in the butter until crumbly. In a small bowl, beat egg and milk; stir into flour mixture just until moistened. Fill eight greased muffin cups ⅔ full. Bake at 425 degrees for 12 minutes, or until golden. Remove from the pan to cool on a wire rack. Just before serving, split and fill with strawberries and top with whipped cream.

My husband's Grandmother Sleeper was an excellent cook; she used to make these English muffins weekly to sell. During our summer vacations to Florida to visit her years ago, she would make us egg and muffin sandwiches from these. I don't make them often because they are so good that we can't stop eating them!

Grammy Sleeper's English Muffins

3 tablespoons butter
1 ¼ teaspoons salt
2 tablespoons sugar
1 cup milk, scalded
1 yeast cake
¼ cup lukewarm water
1 egg, beaten
4 cups sifted flour

Add butter, salt, and sugar to milk and cool to lukewarm. Soften yeast in water. Add yeast, egg, and 2 cups of flour to cooled milk. Stir to blend well, and then knead in remaining flour until firm and elastic. Let rise until doubled in bulk, about 1 hour. Roll out ¼-inch thick on floured board. Cut into 4-inch circles. Leave on board. Cover and let rise until doubled in bulk, about 1 hour. When light, sprinkle with cornmeal, if desired, and bake slowly on a hot, ungreased, heavy griddle or frying pan about 7 minutes on each side. Brown slowly. Makes 12 muffins. I use an electric griddle at almost 300 degrees. Cook for 12 minutes on each side or until done.

Since my mother worked as a hairdresser in our home and had little time to cook, she used this next recipe often so we would have homemade rolls for supper without taking a lot of time.

90 Minute Rolls

1 yeast cake or 1 envelope dry yeast dissolved in ⅓ cup lukewarm water
½ cup lukewarm milk
½ teaspoon salt
2 tablespoons melted shortening
1 tablespoon sugar
2 cups all-purpose flour

Dissolve yeast in lukewarm water. Heat milk to lukewarm; add salt, sugar, melted shortening (use oil if you wish), and dissolved yeast. Stir to mix well. Measure flour into a measuring cup by spoonfuls without sifting. Stir well, cover, and let rise 50 minutes. Stir dough until it falls, then place onto lightly floured board or wax paper. Make into rolls, then place in greased 8-inch pan. Cover and let rise for 20 minutes. Bake at 400 degrees for 20 minutes. Makes 1 dozen rolls.

Steve's mother gave me the following French bread recipe about 35 years ago, which she used to make for her family. I used to make it quite often.

Carolyn's French Bread

Mix together:

1 package dry yeast
1½ cups very warm water
1 tablespoon sugar
1½ teaspoons salt

Add:

1 tablespoon soft shortening or oil
4 cups flour

Stir all together. Mix by hand every 10 minutes 6 times. No kneading! Rest dough 10 minutes after dividing into 2 equal parts. Roll each into a 10" x 8" rectangle; roll up as you would a jellyroll. Slash tops, then sprinkle with cornmeal. Let rise 1 ½ hours. Bake on a lightly greased cookie sheet, being careful not to let loaves touch, at 400 degrees for 30 to 35 minutes. Makes two loaves. After taking from the oven, brush tops with melted butter.

Steve's Aunt Al always brought these cheese rolls to family gatherings and they were a hit. They are easy to make. Often I would use my own refrigerator dough or you can use dough you make in your bread machine rather than to buy frozen bread dough.

Aunt Al's Cheese Rolls

Three loaves of frozen bread dough, or enough bread dough to make about 2 dozen rolls. Let frozen dough thaw, oil top, then let rise to double in size. Pinch off dough for each roll and flatten with fingers. Place a heaping teaspoon of shredded sharp cheddar cheese, (yellow looks the best) in center and turn in to form a ball. Place each roll on a greased cookie sheet. Let rise. Bake at 400 degrees for approximately 20 minutes. These are very basic instructions. I don't think Aunt Al ever used a written recipe for these.

Buttermilk Yeast Rolls

1 package active dry yeast
¼ cup warm (110–115°) water
3 cups buttermilk, room temperature
½ cup sugar
½ cup butter, melted
2 eggs, beaten
1 teaspoon baking soda
1 teaspoon salt
about 8 cups all-purpose flour

Dissolve yeast into warm water in large mixing bowl, stirring to dissolve. Add the buttermilk and sugar; let mixture stand 15 minutes. Mix in warm butter and eggs. Sift soda and salt with 4 cups flour; add to liquid mixture. Beat until smooth batter forms. Add remaining sifted flour, stirring with spoon until dough is no longer sticky. Knead on a floured board, then place in large greased mixing bowl. Cover; let rise until double, about 1 hour. Punch dough down; form into rolls about the size of an egg. Place on greased baking sheet; flatten slightly with your hand. Let rise until double, about 30 minutes. Bake at 350 degrees for 15 to 20 minutes, or until light golden brown. Remove to cooling rack; brush tops with melted butter. Makes about 4 dozen rolls.

My friend Betty Mason is retired now, but worked for years as a cook. She was a school cook and then the head cook in a local nursing home. This next recipe is one that she used often at the nursing home.

Betty's Oatmeal Bread or Rolls

Dissolve 2 packages of dry yeast in ½ cup of warm water.

In a large bowl, mix:

1 cup quick oatmeal
1½ cups boiling water
2 teaspoons salt
2 tablespoons sugar

Let cool, then add:

Dissolved yeast in water
⅛ cup cooking oil
½ cup molasses
2 eggs, beaten
5½ cups flour

Mix well together. Turn out on floured board and knead well. Put into a greased bowl and refrigerate, covered, for 2 hours. Take out and make into rolls or form into loaf. Let rise again. Bake at 400 degrees for 12 to 18 minutes.

The following recipe of Grammy Sleeper's is a little time intensive; however, it's worth it. Many years ago she used to make these to serve at Christmas. The predominant spice in these is ground cardamom, a rather expensive spice that has a distinctive flavor. I remember she had pans of these all over the kitchen before Christmas.

Danish Pastry

Sprinkle 3 packages yeast over 2 cups warm milk in a bowl. Rest 10 minutes. Sift 4 cups flour with ½ cup sugar and 1 teaspoon salt. Mix well with yeast and milk to form a soft dough.

Roll out on a floured board to about ¼" thick. Spread with 1 cup butter or margarine and 1 teaspoon ground cardamom. Fold over and refold. *Do not knead*. Cover and rest 30 minutes.

Roll out and cut into strips. Make into bows, braids, or whatever you prefer. Place on baking sheets. Brush with beaten egg and let rise. Bake at 400 degrees for 15 or 20 minutes. Make sure you watch closely, since you may have to bake at a reduced temperature. Due to the butter or margarine content, they seem to burn easily on the bottom, baking on parchment paper would prevent this. Cool on a wire rack. Place a dollop of jam in the center and drizzle with a glaze. Makes approximately 36 pastries.

Low-Fat Orange Pineapple Muffins

2 cups flour
½ cup brown sugar
1 teaspoon baking powder
½ teaspoon baking soda
½ teaspoon salt
¾ cup low-fat buttermilk
½ cup crushed pineapple, not drained
2 egg whites
2 tablespoons canola oil
1 teaspoon grated orange peel

Preheat oven to 400 degrees. Spray muffin pan with nonstick cooking spray. Combine buttermilk, pineapple, egg whites, oil, brown sugar, and orange peel. Add sifted dry ingredients. Stir just until moistened. Do not overmix because it will make them tough! Divide batter evenly among 12 regular-sized muffin cups or 6 large muffin cups. Bake at 400 degrees for 18 to 22 minutes or until toothpick inserted in muffin comes out clean. Remove from pan and cool on wire rack.

Slow Cooker Boston Brown Bread

1 cup flour
½ cup yellow cornmeal
½ teaspoon baking powder
½ cup whole-wheat flour
1 teaspoon baking soda
½ cup dark molasses
½ teaspoon salt
1 ¼ cups sour milk

Combine flour, baking powder, soda, and salt. Stir in cornmeal and whole-wheat flour. Add molasses and sour milk; beat well.

Pour batter into a greased and floured 2-pound coffee can. Pour a cup of water into Crock-Pot, set can inside. Place aluminum foil over top of can. Cover and bake on high for 2 hours 45 minutes. Slice and serve. Nuts or raisins can be added to the batter if desired. Hint: To sour milk, add 1 teaspoon vinegar to each cup of milk.

Popovers

1 cup flour
¼ teaspoon salt
1 cup milk (room temperature)
1 tablespoon melted butter
2 eggs (room temperature)

Preheat oven to 450 degrees. Grease popover cups or muffin pan and preheat in oven for 4 minutes. Sift flour and salt. Beat eggs, milk, butter, and dry ingredients. Beat until smooth (I use an electric mixer). Pour batter into hot cups until ⅔ full. Bake at 450 degrees for 20 minutes. Reduce heat to 350 degrees for 15 minutes. Puncture each with a toothpick to allow steam to escape as soon as you remove from oven. Makes 6 large popovers.

The following recipe is one that Grammy Sleeper gave me. It is nice to go to my recipe box and pull out a recipe that was handwritten by her. She was known for her good bread-making skills.

All-Bran Brown Bread

1 cup All-Bran cereal
1 cup of sour milk
½ cup raisins
½ cup sugar
1 cup flour
1 teaspoon baking soda
¼ teaspoon salt
1 tablespoon molasses

Mix All-Bran cereal, sour milk, and raisins. Add molasses,

sugar, and flour after sifting with soda and salt. Put into greased bread pan, cover with foil tightly, and steam for 3 hours. To do this in the oven, place filled bread pan in 9" X 13" baking pan filled with 1 ½ inches hot water. Bake for 3 hours at 250 degrees. Grammy Sleeper wrote that she always doubled or tripled this recipe. She also wrote that it was good cold when spread with cream cheese or made into sandwiches using parsley butter or cheese, olives, and nuts.

Date Buttermilk Oatmeal Muffins

2 cups quick-cooking oats
2 cups buttermilk
2 eggs, beaten
1 cup brown sugar
½ cup vegetable oil
2 cups flour
1 teaspoons baking soda
1 teaspoon salt
2 teaspoons baking powder
chopped dates, 1 cup or more

In a bowl, soak oats in buttermilk for 15 minutes. Stir in eggs, sugar, and oil. Combine flour, baking powder, baking soda, and salt; stir into oat mixture just until moistened. Fill greased muffin cups ¾ full. Bake at 400 degrees for 20 to 25 minutes or until muffins test done. Makes 12 jumbo muffins, or 16 regular-sized muffins. If making regular-sized muffins, reduce cooking time to 16 to 18 minutes. These are so yummy.

My favorite biscuit recipe is made with a leavening agent called Bakewell Cream, which is manufactured in Maine.

It causes the biscuits to rise nice and high. I use the recipe on the side of the can. If you can find this product I would highly recommend using it, but if you don't have any available, use the following recipe.

Mile High Biscuits

3 cups flour
¾ teaspoon salt
¼ cup sugar
4 teaspoons baking powder
½ teaspoon cream of tartar
½ cup shortening
1 egg
1⅛ cups milk

Combine all dry ingredients, then cut in shortening; add egg and milk. Mix until a ball forms. Knead on floured board 10 or 12 times. Roll to ¾ inch and cut into biscuits. Bake on greased pan at 425 degrees for 12 to 15 minutes.

Baked French Toast

1 loaf French bread, cut into 1-inch thick slices
8 eggs
3 cups whole milk or half and half
1 ½ teaspoons maple flavoring
2 to 3 tablespoons margarine or butter
2 cups brown sugar

Spray a 9" x 13" pan with cooking spray. Sprinkle 2 cups brown sugar over bottom of pan. Place sliced, buttered bread over the top of the brown sugar in a single layer. Beat 8 eggs, 3 cups of milk, and maple flavoring. Pour over bread slices. Cover with aluminum foil and refrigerate overnight. Remove from refrigerator 30 minutes prior to baking. Bake uncovered at 350 degrees for 1 hour or until golden. Makes 6 to 8 generous servings. No need for syrup!

Hazelnut or French Vanilla Scones

4 cups flour
½ teaspoon cream of tartar
3 tablespoons sugar
4 teaspoons baking powder
½ teaspoon salt
¾ cup butter-flavored Crisco or cold butter
1 egg, separated
1½ cups refrigerated hazelnut or French vanilla nondairy creamer (fat-free is okay)

In a bowl, combine the first five ingredients; cut in Crisco until crumbly. Pour nondairy creamer into a 2-cup measuring cup, whisking in egg yolk. Add to dry ingredients just until moistened, adding more creamer if necessary. Turn onto floured surface and knead 10 times. Divide dough in half. Pat each portion into a 7-inch circle. Cut into eight portions, I use a pizza cutter! Separate wedges and place on greased or parchment paper lined baking pan.

Beat egg white and brush over dough. Sprinkle with sugar. Place oven rack in center of oven. Bake at 475 degrees for 7 minutes. Turn off heat and leave in oven for approximately 5 to 10 minutes or until light golden brown.

This next recipe makes easy caramel rolls that are tender but not heavy. It makes a large amount (two 9" x 13" pans), which allows you to keep some and give the others away! They also freeze well.

Easy Caramel Rolls

2 packages yeast
1 box yellow cake mix
5 cups flour

In a large bowl dissolve yeast in 2½ cups warm water. Add the cake mix and flour. Stir well but don't knead. Cover and set in warm place until doubled in size. Cut dough in half, letting one half of the dough rest while working with the other. On a floured surface, roll dough out into a large rectangle; spread with **soft butter, sugar,** and **cinnamon,** then roll up as a jellyroll.

While preheating oven to 375 degrees, melt ½ cup **butter** for each 9" X 13" baking pan. When melted, sprinkle 1 cup **brown sugar,** and 1 cup **broken walnuts** or **pecans** evenly into pan. Cut the dough into 2-inch slices and arrange on top of this mixture, cut side down. Cover; let rise until double in size (they should be touching each other when ready to bake). Bake until slightly brown, about 20 to 25 minutes. Turn out onto serving tray or heavy-duty aluminum foil. The butter/sugar mixture will drizzle down through the rolls, so turn the rolls out on whatever you will be serving or giving them away on. If you turn one pan out on a large piece of foil they can be frozen, thawed, and slightly heated in the same foil package.

The following is my all-time favorite corn bread recipe that I have been using for over 30 years. It makes a large amount and rises nice and high in the pan.

Corn Bread

2 cups flour
2 cups yellow cornmeal
½ cup sugar
8 teaspoons baking powder
1½ teaspoons salt
4 eggs
2 cups milk
½ cup shortening

Preheat oven to 425 degrees. Sift flour with sugar, baking powder, and salt; stir in cornmeal. Add eggs, milk, and shortening. Beat with electric beater just until smooth, about 1 minute. Don't overbeat! Pour into greased 9" x 13" baking pan. Bake at 425 degrees for 30 to 40 minutes, or until toothpick inserted in the middle comes out clean.

Buttermilk Pancakes #2

2½ cups flour
1 teaspoon baking soda
4 teaspoons baking powder
1 teaspoon salt
2 eggs, beaten
2 cups buttermilk or 2 cups reconstituted powdered milk with two teaspoons vinegar added
4 tablespoons vegetable oil
⅓ cup white sugar

Blend eggs, milk, and oil. Blend dry ingredients together. Add to liquids; beat with wire whisk only until all flour is moistened. To save time, combine all of the dry ingredients in a bowl and cover tightly the night before. Combine all liquids in a separate bowl and refrigerate. In the morning, pour the liquid ingredients into the bowl of dry ingredients. Mix together with a wire whisk. Preheat griddle to 350 degrees. Cook until bubbles surface, then turn.

I love muffins and I love chocolate so this next recipe is one I have made a lot. My Amish friends love them as much as I do. I always send some down to them when I make them.

Chocolate, Chocolate Chip Muffins

2 cups flour
1 teaspoon salt
½ cup Dutch process cocoa
4 teaspoons baking powder
1 ⅓ cups sugar
1 cup milk
½ cup vegetable oil
2 eggs
1 cup chocolate chips

Combine flour, sugar, cocoa, baking powder, and salt; add milk, oil, and eggs all at once. Stir only until moistened. Add chocolate chips. Bake at 400 degrees for 20 minutes for regular-sized muffin pans. For large muffin pans, bake at 375 degrees for 25 to 30 minutes or until toothpick comes out clean. Be sure to grease your muffin tin well. Makes 12 regular or 8 large muffins.

I almost always double this recipe. Be very careful not to overbake because the muffins will be dry. These chocolate muffins should taste moist. I freeze leftover muffins in a zipper type freezer bag and take one out of the freezer as I want one. Wrap a large frozen muffin in a paper towel and microwave on high for 50 to 55 seconds, depending on how powerful your microwave is and the size of your muffin. The chocolate chips are nice and soft when the muffin is heated.

Overnight Coffee Cake

¾ cup butter or margarine, softened
1 cup sugar
2 eggs
2 cups unbleached flour
1 teaspoon baking soda
1 teaspoon nutmeg
½ teaspoon salt
1 cup (8 ounces) sour cream
¾ cup packed brown sugar
½ cup chopped nuts
1 teaspoon cinnamon
1½ cups confectioners' sugar
3 tablespoons milk

In a large mixing bowl, cream butter and sugar. Add eggs, one at a time, beating well after each addition. Combine the flour, baking soda, nutmeg, and salt; add to the creamed mixture alternately with sour cream. Pour into a greased 9" x 13" baking pan.

In a small bowl, combine the brown sugar, nuts, and cinnamon, sprinkle over coffee cake. Cover and refrigerate overnight. Remove from the refrigerator 30 minutes before baking. Bake uncovered at 350 degrees for 35 to 40 minutes or until a toothpick inserted near the center comes out clean. Cool on a wire rack for 10 minutes. Combine confectioners' sugar and milk; drizzle over warm coffee cake. Makes 12 to 15 servings.

It seems like I have made the following coffee cake forever. It is high, moist, and keeps well. It's an old-fashioned recipe. It's really my favorite!

Favorite Coffee Cake

3 cups flour
1 ½ cups white sugar
5 teaspoons baking powder
1 ½ teaspoons salt
½ cup shortening
1 ½ cups milk
2 eggs

Heat oven to 375 degrees. Grease a 9" x 13" baking pan. Blend all ingredients, beat vigorously 30 seconds. Spread in pan. Sprinkle topping over batter. Bake 25 to 30 minutes.

Topping:

Mix with a pastry blender:
½ cup packed brown sugar
2 teaspoons cinnamon
2 tablespoons butter or margarine
½ cup finely chopped nuts (optional)

Sprinkle the mixture over the batter. Bake as directed above.

Desserts

The following cake is one that Steve's mother often made. It is a nice spice cake recipe that doesn't hint of the secret ingredient, a can of tomato soup!

Tomato Soup Cake

- ½ cup shortening
- 1 ⅓ cups sugar
- 2 eggs
- 2 cups flour
- 1 tablespoon baking powder
- 1 teaspoon baking soda
- 2 teaspoons allspice
- 1 teaspoon cinnamon
- 1-10 ¾-ounce can condensed tomato soup
- ¼ cup water
- 1 cup chopped walnuts
- ½ cup raisins

Preheat oven to 350 degrees. Grease and flour a Bundt pan or tube pan. In a medium bowl, cream shortening and sugar. Add eggs and beat until fluffy. Sift dry ingredients. Mix tomato soup and water. Add sifted ingredients and soup mixture alternately to creamed mixture. Fold in nuts and raisins. Pour into pan. Frost with peanut butter, white, or cream cheese frosting after cooling.

My Amish friend Miriam is a very good cook and always so generous. One day she brought me a 10-pound free-range, fresh-plucked chicken. She had spent the morning killing and dressing her chickens. I'm sure I will never have one fresher than hers.

I asked her if I could have one of her favorite recipes and she gave me the following.

Apple Roll

2 cups flour
3 teaspoons baking powder
½ teaspoon salt
2 tablespoons sugar
3 tablespoons lard
1 beaten egg
¾ cup milk
7 apples

Combine all ingredients, roll out and spread 7 sliced, peeled apples, 2 tablespoons sugar, and ¾ teaspoon cinnamon on dough, then roll it up and slice it. Place in cake pan and bake in a syrup of 1 ½ cups brown sugar and ¾ cup hot water. Bake at 350 degrees.

Miriam says that she always uses real maple syrup in this recipe, more maple syrup than brown sugar and water. No time given. She states this is very good with ice cream or milk. My raspberry roll recipe is similar to this apple roll and I bake it for 10 minutes at 425 degrees and then at 350 for 20 minutes, using an electric oven.

Sarah and I just love the following date recipe. My mother used it for years.

Date Crumbs

Mix:

   2 cups flour
   2 cups quick or regular oats
   1 cup brown sugar
   1 teaspoon baking soda
   dash of salt
   ¾ cup butter

Pat half of this mixture into a greased 9" x 13" pan, then cook the following ingredients until thick:

   1-8-ounce package chopped dates
   1 cup boiling water
   ½ cup white sugar
   1 teaspoon vanilla
   2 tablespoons flour

Spread this mixture over the crumbs. Add the other half of crumbs over the top and bake at 400 degrees until brown.

Apples are plentiful in Maine in the fall. The next recipe is one that I have used often because the squares are so moist and flavorful.

Baked Apple Squares

   1¾ cups white sugar
   3 eggs

Beat well, then add:

   2 cups flour
   1 teaspoon baking powder
   1 teaspoon cinnamon

½ teaspoon salt
1 teaspoon vanilla
1 scant cup cooking oil
1 cup chopped nuts, optional
2 cups very thinly sliced McIntosh apples

Fold in peeled and sliced apples and nuts last. Bake in a greased 9" X 13" pan at 350 degrees for 40 to 50 minutes.

Chocolate Chip Squares

Cream together:

1 cup shortening
½ cup brown sugar
½ cup white sugar

Add:

2 eggs, slightly beaten
1 tablespoon cold water
1 teaspoon vanilla

Then add (sifted together):

2 cups flour
1 teaspoon baking soda
¼ teaspoon salt

Spread evenly onto a greased cookie sheet. Beat 2 egg whites until stiff. Gradually add:

1 cup brown sugar
6 ounces chocolate chips

Smooth on top of first mixture. Bake at 350 degrees for 25 minutes.

I'm not sure where I first got the following recipe; I think it was from Steve's mother. I know I entered it in one of the first editions of the Albion cookbooks, nearly 35 years ago. It's very inexpensive to make and very moist.

Oatmeal Cake

1½ cups boiling water poured over 1 cup quick oatmeal

Set aside. Cream together:

½ cup shortening
1 cup white sugar
1 cup brown sugar

Beat in **2 eggs**, then add:

1 ⅓ cups flour
1 teaspoon cinnamon
1 teaspoon baking soda
½ teaspoon salt

Beat well and add oatmeal mixture. Bake at 350 degrees for 35 to 40 minutes in a greased 9" x 13" pan.

Frosting:

¾ stick margarine
¾ cup brown sugar
1 tablespoon milk

Mix and boil 1 minute. Add:

1 cup coarsely chopped nuts
1 cup flaked coconut

Spread onto cake. Put under broiler for a few minutes, watching closely!

I know I got the following recipe from my mother-in-law, Carolyn. I first had it at her house before I was married. It's economical and very moist. Often I didn't have buttermilk so I soured milk with 1 teaspoon vinegar per 1 cup milk.

Texas Sheet Cake

Put in a saucepan and bring to a boil:

1 stick margarine
½ cup cooking oil
4 tablespoons cocoa
1 cup water

Sift together:

2 cups flour
2 cups white sugar

Pour first mixture over second mixture and mix well. Beat **2 eggs** and add:

½ cup buttermilk (or sour milk)
1 teaspoon baking soda
1 teaspoon vanilla

Add to batter and pour into greased cookie sheet with sides. Bake at 400 degrees for 20 minutes. Frost cake while still hot.

Frosting:

Bring to a boil:

1 stick margarine
⅓ cup buttermilk or sour milk
4 tablespoons cocoa

Remove from heat. Add:

1 pound confectioners' sugar
1 teaspoon vanilla
½ teaspoon salt
1 cup chopped nuts (optional)
Spread on warm cake.

I remember my mother making this next recipe when I was young. Probably the recipe was developed either during the Depression or during wartime.

Cheap Fruit Cake

1 cup sugar
1 teaspoon cinnamon, cloves, and nutmeg
2 cups flour
½ cup lard (shortening) or butter
1 egg
½ cup raisins and ½ cup chopped nuts
1 cup buttermilk in which 1 teaspoon of baking soda has been dissolved
½ teaspoon salt

There were no instructions with this recipe. I would mix well and pour into a greased 8" x 8" pan. Bake at 350 degrees about 20 minutes or when toothpick comes out clean.

When I was very young we didn't have the nice fresh fruits available in Maine at a reasonable price like we do now. Most people canned peaches, pears, and made their own apple-sauce for the winter months when fresh fruit was scarce. My mother would often give us canned fruit, which was often fruit cocktail. It was a pantry staple back then and made a very moist, flavorful cake.

Fruit Cocktail Cake

2 cups sifted flour
2 eggs
2 teaspoons baking soda
1-16-ounce can fruit cocktail
½ teaspoon salt
1 ½ cups white sugar
½ or 1 cup chopped nuts
1 cup brown sugar

Blend flour, soda, salt, white sugar, eggs, and fruit cocktail together. Pour mixture into a well-greased and floured 9"x13" pan. Sprinkle chopped nuts and top with brown sugar. Bake at 350 degrees for 40 minutes.

My Favorite Piecrust

2 cups flour
½ teaspoon salt
⅔ to ¾ cup shortening
about ¼ to ⅓ cup ice water

Mix flour, shortening, and salt together using a pastry

blender. When well blended, add ice water a little at a time until mixture just sticks together, but not wet. Too much water makes the piecrust tough. This recipe makes enough for a 10-inch double piecrust. For two baked 10-inch pie shells, bake at 475 degrees for 8 to 10 minutes. When baking just the pie shells, make sure you prick the bottom and sides of the piecrust well or it will shrink into the dish during baking.

I remember being a teenager and walking home from our church youth group meeting every Monday evening with my sister, arriving home to some kind of dessert. Pineapple pie was one dessert I remember Mom making often.

One-Crust Pineapple Pie

1 cup crushed pineapple
3 tablespoons flour
1 cup white sugar
1 cup water
2 egg yolks
dash of salt

Combine all ingredients and cook in the top of a double boiler until thickened.

Pour into a 9-inch baked pie shell. Spread with meringue to edge. Bake in oven until meringue is golden brown. Watch closely, meringue browns quickly.

The following blueberry pie recipe is different from any I have seen before; it has brown sugar instead of white sugar. My son Andy loves this pie and I have to say it's the best blueberry pie recipe that I have tried. Using Maine's small blueberries also makes this pie extra good.

Blueberry Pie

pastry for a 2-crust 9-inch pie
3½ cups blueberries
3 tablespoons flour
1 cup packed light brown sugar
2 tablespoons margarine

Mix first three ingredients and put in pastry-lined 9-inch pie plate. Dot with margarine and adjust top crust. Bake in hot oven (400 degrees) about 35 minutes. Serve slightly warm or cool.

My favorite type of chocolate chip cookies are called cowboy cookies, but when we were in Honduras I didn't have that recipe with me for the first few months. The only chocolate chips I could find in the city were the Baker's brand, which had a chocolate chip cookie recipe on the back of the package. I used this recipe regularly when I could actually find the chocolate chips to purchase. My favorite thing to cook is chocolate chip cookies; it is a comfort food for me, even in the heat and humidity of a tropical climate. I think I must have introduced the local children and our armed guards to chocolate chip cookies for the first time. I'm not sure if that was good, though!

Baker's Chocolate Chip Cookies

1 cup (2 sticks) butter or margarine, softened
2 ¼ cups flour

¾ cup white sugar (only brown was available in
Honduras)
¾ cup firmly packed brown sugar
1 teaspoon baking soda
¼ teaspoon salt
2 eggs
1 teaspoon vanilla
1 cup chopped nuts (optional)
1-12-ounce package chocolate chips

Heat oven to 375 degrees. Beat butter, sugars, eggs, and vanilla in large bowl with electric mixer on medium speed until light and fluffy. Mix in flour, baking soda, and salt. Stir in chips and nuts. Drop by teaspoonfuls 2 inches apart onto ungreased cooking sheets. Bake 10 minutes or until golden brown. Remove from cookie sheets and cool on wire racks. Makes about 6 dozen cookies.

Cowboy Cookies

2 sticks butter or margarine
1 cup sugar
1 cup packed brown sugar
1 teaspoon vanilla
2 eggs
2 cups sifted flour
1 teaspoon baking soda
½ teaspoon baking powder
½ teaspoon salt
2 cups uncooked quick oatmeal
1 cup chocolate chips

Cream butter, sugar, and vanilla. Beat until smooth and

creamy. Add eggs one at a time, beating well after each addition. Sift dry ingredients together. Add sifted ingredients to creamed mixture. Stir in the uncooked oats and then the chocolate chips. Drop by teaspoonfuls onto greased or parchment paper-lined cookie sheets. Bake at 350 degrees for about 10 to 12 minutes. Makes about 7 dozen cookies. I usually double this recipe and freeze half. You can form the dough into rolls on waxed paper, wrap in aluminum foil and freeze to bake at another time. This cookie dough tastes great!

Pecan Pie

3 eggs, slightly beaten
1 teaspoon vanilla
1 cup light corn syrup
1 cup white sugar
2 tablespoons melted butter or margarine
1¼ cups pecan halves or more
1-9-inch unbaked piecrust

Preheat oven to 350 degrees. In a large bowl stir first 5 ingredients with wire whisk until well blended. Stir in pecans, pour into piecrust. Bake 50 to 55 minutes or until knife inserted in center (or halfway to center) comes out clean. Don't overbake! Cool.

My daughter-in-law Stacy is a wonderful cook. Everything she makes looks perfect, including the following mint-frosted brownies. They also taste so good! I have used another recipe similar to this, but hers is the best.

Mint-Frosted Brownies

Brownies:

4 eggs
2 cups sugar
½ teaspoon salt
2 teaspoons vanilla
4 squares unsweetened chocolate, melted and cooled slightly
1 cup oil
1 ⅓ cups sifted flour
1 cup chopped nuts (optional)

Beat eggs, sugar, and vanilla. Add chocolate and oil. Beat. Fold in flour and nuts, then spread in a greased and floured 9" x 13" pan. Bake at 350 degrees for 25 to 30 minutes.

Frosting:

1 pound confectioners' sugar, sifted
½ cup butter, softened
1 teaspoon vanilla
3 tablespoons milk (use more as needed)

Beat together. Add peppermint extract to taste. Add green food coloring to desired color.

Chocolate glaze:

4 to 6 squares unsweetened chocolate
3 tablespoons butter
1 ½ cups confectioners' sugar

2 to 3 tablespoons hot water

Melt chocolate and butter. Stir in confectioners' sugar. Add water to desired consistency. Spread over green layer.

I do not use unsweetened baking chocolate, except for Christmas candy making. It's too expensive. I prefer to use cocoa that I purchase in bulk and always have on hand. The following is the best chocolate brownie recipe that I have tried, that makes a 9" x 13" pan.

Chocolate Brownies

2 sticks (1 cup) margarine
4 eggs
2 cups white sugar
¾ cup cocoa
1 ¼ cups flour
¼ teaspoon salt
1 teaspoon vanilla

Preheat oven to 350 degrees. Melt the margarine in the microwave on high for about 45 seconds using the same bowl you will be mixing the brownies in. Add the slightly beaten eggs and vanilla into the slightly cooled melted margarine. Mix together the cocoa and sugar, then add to the butter. Add the sifted flour and salt last. Mix well, then spread the mixture evenly into the 9" x 13" greased baking pan. Bake for 40 to 50 minutes. Don't overbake! Brownies are done when a toothpick comes out clean about an inch or two from the side of the pan.

This next recipe is so quick and easy. It is very moist and a great dessert for serving to guests, which I did a lot while living in Honduras. Try to buy canned pumpkin if you don't freeze your own. I buy several cans around Christmas and Thanksgiving when the price is nearly half what it is the rest of the year. I think I found this recipe in a *Country Woman* magazine.

Pumpkin Cake with Caramel Sauce

2 cups flour
½ teaspoon salt
2 cups white sugar
2 teaspoons baking soda
2 teaspoons ground cinnamon
1 teaspoon ground nutmeg
4 eggs
1-16-ounce can solid pack pumpkin
1 cup vegetable oil

In a mixing bowl, combine the first six ingredients. In another bowl, beat eggs, pumpkin, and oil until smooth; add to the dry ingredients. Mix until well blended, about 1 minute. Pour into a greased 9" x 13" baking pan. Bake at 350 degrees for 35 to 40 minutes or until a wooden toothpick inserted near the center comes out clean. Cool on a wire rack.

Caramel Sauce

1 ½ cups packed brown sugar
3 tablespoons flour
pinch of salt
1 ¼ cups water
2 tablespoons butter or margarine

½ teaspoon vanilla

For sauce, combine brown sugar, flour, and salt in a saucepan. Stir in water and butter; bring to a boil over medium heat. Boil for 3 minutes, stirring constantly. Remove from heat; stir in vanilla. Cut cake into squares and serve with warm sauce. Makes 12 to 15 servings. I like to serve this cake cooled and topped with vanilla ice cream and warm caramel sauce.

The following is another of Grammy Sleeper's recipes that she gave me a couple of years before she died. She said that she got it from a friend from the state of Washington.

Judy's Birthday Cake

1 package yellow cake mix with pudding added
1 can of mandarin oranges with the juice
4 eggs
½ cup oil

Beat ingredients together for 4 minutes. Pour into 2 greased and floured 9-inch pans. Bake at 350 degrees for 30 to 35 minutes. Cool and slice each layer in half.

Mix together:

1 large container of whipped topping (5 ½ cups)
1 large package of vanilla instant pudding
1-20-ounce can crushed pineapple, including the juice

Mix together whipped topping and pudding mix. Add the

pineapple and juice. Use this between cake layers and for frosting top and sides of cake. Refrigerate at least 3 hours.

My mother made a very good piecrust; however, she never used a recipe. Several years ago, I asked her if she would put all of her piecrust ingredients in a bowl and then take them out and measure, which she did. A nice tip if you are young and starting to collect recipes is to have the recipe handwritten by the person giving it to you, with their name written on it. Even though Steve's mother and grandmother and my mother are now deceased, I have some of their favorite recipes handwritten by them!

Mom's Piecrust

5 cups flour
1 teaspoon salt
2 ¼ cups Crisco shortening
½ to ¾ cup of cold (or ice) water

Blend flour, salt, and shortening with pastry blender until the consistency of small peas. Add cold water until it holds together. This makes about 3 double-crust pies.

The following is probably my favorite bar recipe. My friend Lynne gave it to me years ago. I have made quite a few copies of this recipe, because I can always count on at least one person requesting it each time I take it to a new gathering. I usually keep a box of yellow cake mix on hand for several recipes I like to use. The store brand works well in this recipe. I can always find cake mixes from 75 cents to a dollar.

Ooey-Gooey Butter Bars

Bottom:

1 egg
1 stick butter, melted
1 box yellow cake mix (2-layer size)

Mix together and pat dough into a greased 9"x 13" pan.

Top:

2 eggs
1 pound confectioners' sugar
1 teaspoon almond extract
1-8-ounce package softened cream cheese

Beat well pour over patted cake mix. Sprinkle with ½ cup walnuts or pecans, chopped fine. Bake at 350 degrees for 40 minutes. Dust with confectioners' sugar after removing from oven. Cool at least 2 hours before cutting.

I just love to make cookies. The following recipe is another one of my favorite cookie recipes. It makes a very large batch. I remember when Chris was in high school his friends liked to eat these as much as I liked making them! These are moist cookies. Be careful not to over bake.

Ginger Krinkles

1 ½ cups margarine or butter, softened
2 cups brown sugar
½ cup molasses
2 eggs
5 cups flour
4 teaspoons baking soda

2 teaspoons cinnamon
1 to 2 teaspoons ginger
1 teaspoon ground cloves
sugar

Cream butter with brown sugar, molasses, and eggs until well mixed. Combine flour, baking soda, cinnamon, ginger, and cloves; add to creamed mixture and mix well. Chill until dough can be handled easily, about 2 hours.

Preheat oven to 350 degrees. Form dough into 1-inch balls; roll each ball in sugar to coat well. Place balls 3 inches apart on cookie sheets. Bake 8 to 10 minutes until set but not browned. Makes 6 to 8 dozen.

The following is a very basic sugar cookie recipe that I got with Tupperware cookie cutters at least 35 years ago. I've used other sugar cookie recipes, but I always go back to this one.

Granny's Sugar Cookies

Cream together:

½ cup butter or margarine
1 cup sugar
Blend in **1 large egg**.
Sift together and add to mixture:
2 to 2 ¼ cups all-purpose flour
2 teaspoons baking powder
½ teaspoon salt
½ teaspoon vanilla

Divide dough into two parts. Chill 1 to 2 hours so it will be easy to handle. Roll dough, one part at a time, to ⅛-inch thickness and cut with a cookie cutter lightly dusted with flour. Keep the other portion of dough chilled until ready to roll. Transfer cookies to cookie sheet and bake in preheated 350-degree oven 8 to 10 minutes. Frost with confectioners' sugar glaze. Makes 2 dozen cookies.

Confectioners' Glaze:

Blend together 1 cup confectioners' sugar and 5 to 6 teaspoons water. Add food coloring, if desired. Brush glaze over cookies while still warm.

Sarah loves the following recipe. She would usually request it as a birthday cake, although it looks more like frosted brownies. I sometime use the cake portion of this recipe to make brownies, which are very moist and fudgey!

Mississippi Mud Cake

2 sticks margarine
2 cups sugar
1½ cups sifted flour
½ cup cocoa
dash of salt
1 cup pecans (optional)
4 eggs, beaten
2 teaspoons vanilla
1-7-ounce jar marshmallow fluff

Melt margarine and pour into a large bowl. Add sifted dry ingredients and nuts. Add eggs and vanilla, mixing well. Pour mixture into 9" x 13" greased pan and bake for 30 to

35 minutes at 350 degrees. Immediately after taking out of oven, spread with one jar of marshmallow fluff. Then top with icing.

Icing:

> **½ stick margarine**
> **½ cup cocoa**
> **6 tablespoons milk**
> **1 pound confectioners' sugar**

Melt margarine; add cocoa, milk, and sugar. Beat and spread over marshmallow cream layer. We think this cake is better served cold from the refrigerator. It's very rich and gooey!

Brownie Pie

> **1 cup chocolate chips**
> **1 stick butter, melted**
> **1 cup chopped pecans**
> **1 teaspoon vanilla**
> **½ cup all-purpose flour**
> **½ cup white sugar**
> **½ cup brown sugar**
> **2 eggs, beaten**

Pour warm butter over chocolate chips and stir. Blend all remaining ingredients and stir into chocolate chip mixture. Pour into unbaked pie shell. Bake in 350-degree oven for 30 to 40 minutes. Serve with whipped cream or ice cream.

Strawberry Cake

1 package white cake mix
1 package strawberry gelatin
½ cup cold water
4 eggs
½ cup cooking oil
½ cup frozen sweetened strawberries

Mix and add 4 eggs, one at a time. Bake 35 to 40 minutes at 350 degrees in a 9" x 13" greased pan. Serve with whipped cream and remaining strawberries. Makes 24 servings.

I think the following brownie recipe is the one my mother used to make a lot when I was growing up. I remember that it sure was yummy! Her baking day was usually Monday afternoons since that was her day off during the week. She would make several desserts to last the week. Sometimes these brownies are called blonde brownies.

Brown Sugar Brownies

⅔ cup melted butter or margarine
1 pound light brown sugar
3 eggs
2 ⅔ cups flour
1 teaspoon salt
2 teaspoons baking powder
1-6-ounce package chocolate chips
½ cup chopped nuts (optional)

Mix melted butter with brown sugar and beaten eggs. Mix in sifted dry ingredients. Add chocolate chips and nuts with the flour mixture. Bake at 350 degrees F. for about 30 minutes. Don't overcook! This is an old recipe that didn't include a baking time. I think it's around 30 minutes so watch closely! This should be baked in a 9" x 13" greased baking pan.

The following is a recipe my husband's Grandmother Sleeper gave me years ago. The recipe calls for butter, but I always used margarine. My sister at Christmastime makes a similar recipe that always tastes so much better than mine. It wasn't until recently that I discovered why. She says that she always uses real butter in her recipe. It really makes a difference!

Heath Bars

1 cup butter, no substitutions
1 cup brown sugar
1-12-ounce package chocolate chips or 1 cup chopped nuts

Line a cookie sheet with aluminum foil. Coat lightly with nonstick cooking spray. Line with saltine or graham crackers. Boil butter and sugar hard for 2 ½ minutes. Pour over crackers and place in 350-degree oven for 5 minutes. Take from oven and pour chocolate chips over the crackers. They will melt, then spread evenly to coat all of the crackers. Cool in the refrigerator. Break up and store in an airtight container. I think these are great without the chocolate chips. My sister makes them with walnuts or pecans instead of chocolate chips. I like hers better. If using the nuts, add them to the sugar mixture just before pouring onto crackers.

O'Henry Bars

    1 cup brown sugar
    ½ cup butter
    ⅛ cup milk
    1 egg

Bring above ingredients to boil and add **1 cup graham crackers (crushed), 1 cup walnuts (chopped),** and **1 cup coconut.**

Pour over **9 graham crackers** in a 9" x 9" pan. Place another **9 graham crackers** over that. Press gently. Frost with a butter icing and sprinkle with graham cracker crumbs.

I love the following raspberry roll recipe, but I think I only ever made it during raspberry season in Maine, which is in early July. When I think of fresh raspberry season, I think of this once-a-year dessert! One year when I was trying to be very frugal, my young children and I went out in the woods within walking distance from our house to pick wild raspberries that were very plentiful. Naïvely, we went the day after a heavy rain. We picked a couple of buckets of berries, but the berries were filled with water and became mushy very quickly. They also became moldy quickly, even though they were stored in the refrigerator. Don't pick raspberries right after a heavy rain!

Raspberry Roll

    1 cup fresh raspberries
    butter
    ½ cup sugar
    2 cups sifted flour

1 teaspoon salt
4 teaspoons baking powder
2 rounded tablespoons shortening
2 tablespoons sugar
⅞ cup milk

Sift flour, salt, baking powder, and 2 tablespoons sugar into bowl. Cut in shortening. Add milk slowly. Roll out this dough to ½-inch thickness. Dot the dough with bits of butter. Cover dough with fresh berries. Sprinkle berries with ½ cup sugar. Roll as for a jellyroll. Cut into ½-inch slices, making 10 to 12 slices. Spray 9" x 13" baking pan with nonstick spray. Place slices in pan, then pour the following syrup over slices after boiling.

1 cup sugar
1 tablespoon flour
Dash of salt
1 tablespoon butter
1 cup water
1 teaspoon vanilla

Measure sugar, flour ,and salt into a saucepan. Stir. Add water slowly. Add butter and bring to a boil, boil for 3 minutes. Add vanilla and pour over the slices. Bake for 10 minutes at 425 degrees, then for 20 minutes at 350 degrees. Serve warm, topped with whipped topping or ice cream.

Hurry-Up Caramel Cake

Preheat oven to 350 degrees. Grease and lightly flour two 9-inch round layer pans. Stir together in a large mixing bowl, pressing out lumps with the back of a spoon:

½ cup white sugar
1 cup light brown sugar
Stir into the sugars:
2 ¼ cups all-purpose flour
1 teaspoon salt
1 tablespoon baking powder

Add and mix at low speed until the dry ingredients are moistened. Beat at medium speed until smooth:

8 tablespoons softened butter
1 cup milk
Scrape bowl and beaters. Add and beat at low speed:
2 large eggs
1 ¼ teaspoons vanilla

Beat again at medium speed until smooth. Fill cake pans and bake at 350 degrees for 30 minutes, or until the cake begins to pull away from the sides of the pan. Cool in the pans for 8 minutes. Turn out, cool completely, then fill and frost with:

Hurry-Up Caramel Frosting

8 tablespoons butter
1 cup brown sugar
⅛ teaspoon salt
5 ounces evaporated milk

Stir this mixture over medium heat until butter is melted, sugar dissolved, and the surface is covered with bubbles. Remove from heat and add 1 teaspoon vanilla.

Beat in, a ½ cup at a time, about 4 cups of confectioners'

sugar. Stop beating when you get the consistency you desire. Work quickly and frost the cake, as this tends to harden and "sugar up" like pralines. The cake serves 10 to 12 people. This cake is very good, but very rich!

I love the following cookie recipe; however, my children didn't like the raisins or nuts. I have changed the original recipe, which I think tastes just right now!

A Large Batch of Cookies

1 cup water
2 cups raisins

Boil the water and raisins together and let cool.

1 cup margarine or cooking oil
2 cups brown sugar
3 eggs
1 teaspoon vanilla
4 cups all-purpose flour
1 teaspoon baking powder
1 teaspoon baking soda
2 teaspoons salt
1½ teaspoons cinnamon
¼ teaspoon nutmeg
¼ teaspoon allspice
1 cup walnuts, chopped

Combine butter with sugar and beat until there is no "gritty" feeling left. Beat in the eggs and vanilla. Combine all dry ingredients and mix into the shortening mixture alternately with the cooled water and raisins.

Add chopped walnuts and drop on a greased cookie

sheet. Bake in medium oven (350 degree) until light brown, approximately 10 minutes.

I have only made the following recipe once, but because it was so good I just had to include it in my book. It is not necessarily a frugal recipe, but a very special dessert to serve to special guests. Because of its richness it will serve quite a few people since the servings will likely be smaller. For a pretty presentation, try squirting chocolate sauce zigzag over a dessert plate before placing the bar on the plate. You could then dust it lightly with confectioners' sugar.

Buster Bars

Layer 1:

Pack **1 package of crushed Oreo cookies** with **1 stick melted margarine** in a 9"x13" pan.

Layer 2:

Spread **softened half-gallon vanilla ice cream** over first layer.

Layer 3:

12 ounces Spanish peanuts
Freeze first 3 layers.
Layer 4:
Frosting: 2 cups confectioners' sugar
½ cup butter or margarine
12 ounces evaporated milk
1 teaspoon vanilla

⅔ cup chocolate chips

Boil frosting for 8 minutes. Let cool. Spread on ice cream layer. Cover with aluminum foil and keep in freezer until shortly before serving. Makes a good summer-time dessert and can be made ahead.

The following is another very good summer dessert recipe for a large group. The best part is that it can be made way ahead and kept in the freezer. Sometimes I use a different flavor of ice cream. I also like to use the recipe for the chocolate layer as an ice cream topping.

Banana Split Dessert

4 cups graham cracker crumbs mixed with ½ cup melted margarine for crust
2 or 3 bananas
½ gallon Neapolitan ice cream
1 cup chopped walnuts
1 cup chocolate chips
½ cup butter
2 cups confectioners' sugar
1½ cups evaporated milk
1 teaspoon vanilla
1 large tub of frozen whipped topping

Cover bottom of 11" x 15" pan with a graham cracker crust. Reserve 1 cup crumbs. Slice bananas crosswise and layer over crust. Slice ice cream in ½-inch thick slices and place over bananas. Sprinkle ice cream with 1 cup chopped walnuts. Freeze until firm. Melt 1 cup chocolate chips and ½ cup butter; add 2 cups powdered sugar and 1½ cups evaporated milk. Cook mixture until thick and smooth, stirring constantly. Remove from heat and add 1 teaspoon vanilla. Cool chocolate mixture, then pour over ice cream and freeze until firm. Spread softened whipped topping over chocolate layer and top with reserved crumbs. Store in freezer, covered with aluminum foil. Remove about 10 minutes or more before serving. This will keep for several weeks in the freezer. Makes 25 servings.

The following chocolate cake recipe makes a very good triple layer chocolate cake. Frosted with 7-minute boiled frosting and served on a pedestal cake plate, it looks very impressive. Since I buy my cocoa in bulk, and usually have the other ingredients on hand, I can whip up this cake without planning ahead. I do prefer the Dutch cocoa for all of my cocoa recipes. It's darker and richer in flavor. I found this cake recipe in a cookbook entitled, *Mary Jane's Cookbook.*[2]

Chocolate Cake

Mix until smooth then cool:
   1 cup unsifted cocoa
   2 cups boiling water
Mix at high speed for 5 minutes:
   1 cup butter or margarine
   2 ½ cups granulated sugar
   4 eggs
   1 ½ teaspoons vanilla
Sift together:
   2 ¾ cups flour
   1 teaspoon salt
   2 teaspoons baking soda
   ½ teaspoon baking powder

Add dry ingredients alternately with cooled cocoa mixture. Do not overbeat. Divide evenly between 3 greased and floured 9-inch layer cake pans. Bake at 350 degrees for 25 to 30 minutes. Cool in pans for 10 minutes; remove and cool completely on racks.

I have used the following double boiler frosting recipe for years. My husband prefers this frosting to the regular confectioners' sugar icing. It's easy to make and makes a large amount so it's great for frosting a triple layer cake.

Double Boiler 7-Minute Frosting

2 egg whites (¼ cup)
1 ½ cups sugar
¼ teaspoon cream of tartar or 1 tablespoon light corn syrup
⅓ cup water
1 teaspoon vanilla

Combine egg whites, sugar, cream of tartar, and water in top of double boiler. Beat on high speed for 1 minute with electric hand mixer. Place over boiling water, not letting water touch the bottom of the pan. Beat on high speed for 7 minutes. Remove pan from boiling water; add vanilla. Beat 2 minutes longer on high speed. Fills and frosts 2 or 3, 8 or 9-inch layers or generously frosts a 9"x 13" cake.

The next recipe is my favorite blueberry cake recipe. It is very much like a coffeecake. It is very moist and makes a large, high cake. This recipe calls for a lot of blueberries; I use the small Maine blueberries. I always made it each July after my annual trek to buy a flat of blueberries. Now I make it all year long using the ones I freeze.

Blueberry Buckle

Mix:

  1½ cups sugar
  ½ cup shortening
  2 eggs
Stir in:
  1 cup milk.
Add:
  3 ½ cups sifted flour
  1 teaspoon salt
  4 teaspoons baking powder

Add **4 ½ cups blueberries**. Pour into a greased 9" X 13" pan and sprinkle with the following, mixed well with pastry blender:

  1 cup sugar
  1 teaspoon cinnamon
  ⅔ cup flour
  ½ cup soft butter

Bake 50 minutes or until toothpick inserted into the middle comes out clean. Bake in a 9"x 13" pan at 375 degrees. Sometimes I bake this in a sheet cake pan and take it to church for coffee time. It's easier to serve this way and serves more people.

The following recipe is quick to prepare and if you keep a

bottle of lemon juice on hand in your refrigerator, this is a nice dessert to serve company or to use as a party finger food without having to run to the store to buy special ingredients. I took these bars to a ladies Bible study once while I was living in Honduras, thinking it was a clever way to use up lemons that were inexpensive and plentiful there. What I did not realize was that the other ladies used the same recipe for the same reason!

Lemon Fingers

2 cups flour
½ cup confectioners' sugar, plus some for dusting
1 cup butter or margarine
4 eggs
¼ cup lemon juice
2 cups sugar
¼ cup flour

Preheat oven to 350 degrees. Lightly grease a 9" x 13" pan.

In a bowl, sift together 2 cups flour and ½ cup confectioners' sugar. Cut in butter with a pastry blender until mixture resembles coarse meal.

Press mixture in bottom of baking pan. Bake 20 to 25 minutes until lightly browned. Remove from oven.

Meanwhile beat eggs; add sugar, lemon juice, and flour thoroughly. Pour onto browned crust. Bake 15 minutes then dust with confectioners' sugar. Cool completely before cutting. Store in refrigerator.

The following bars are like peanut butter cups. I used to make these bars when I had to take refreshments to a youth group meeting. I usually make these at Christmastime also.

I only make these bars for special occasions because they are so rich. I think my mother first started making these and she always made them at Christmastime.

Peanut Butter Bars

Melt:
2 sticks margarine (1 cup)
2 cups creamy peanut butter
In a large bowl mix:
2 cups confectioners' sugar
2 cups graham cracker crumbs

Two cups of graham cracker crumbs are the equivalent to 1 pack of graham crackers plus 3 ½ squares of crackers crushed into fine crumbs. Use a rolling pin or blender to make the crumbs. If using a rolling pin, put the graham crackers into a plastic bag, which keeps the crumbs contained and the rolling pin clean.

Pour the liquid ingredients into the mixture. Mix until all ingredients are mixed together. Grease a 9" x 13" pan and press peanut butter mixture into it. Add topping.

Topping:
Melt:
1 stick margarine (½ cup)
1-12-ounce bag chocolate chips

Pour over peanut butter bars while chocolate is hot. Let them set at room temperature until hard, then cut into bars.

Hot fudge sundae cake is a quick and easy decadent dessert that can be cooked in the oven with the rest of a meal or quickly in the microwave oven if you don't have your oven on already.

Hot Fudge Sundae Cake

1 cup flour
¾ cup sugar
2 tablespoons cocoa
2 teaspoons baking powder
¼ teaspoon salt
½ cup milk
2 tablespoons cooking oil
¼ teaspoon vanilla
1 cup packed brown sugar
½ cup cocoa
1 ¾ cups hottest tap water

Heat oven to 350 degrees. In ungreased 8-inch square pan, stir together flour, sugar, 2 tablespoons cocoa, baking powder, and salt. Mix in milk, oil, and vanilla with fork until smooth. Spread evenly in pan. Sprinkle with brown sugar and **½ cup cocoa**. Pour hot water over batter. Bake 40 minutes. Let stand 15 minutes. Spoon in dessert dishes, inverting so that sauce is on the top. Top with a scoop of ice cream. Makes 9 servings.

To cook in the microwave:

Measure the 1¾ cups water into a 2-cup glass measuring cup; place in microwave oven to boil, about 4 minutes on high. Substitute an ungreased 2-quart glass casserole for a square pan; pour boiling water over batter in casserole dish.

Cook uncovered 8 to 10 minutes, or until cake is no longer doughy. Let stand a few minutes; spoon into dessert dishes.

My good friend Doreen Marr made this next recipe for my family years ago while we were visiting her in North Carolina. Andy ate so much of it that he has never liked it since! It is very yummy!

Monkey Bread

3 cans canned refrigerated biscuits (30)
melted butter
sugar
cinnamon

I have never had the exact measurements for this recipe. Start with ½ cup melted butter. Stir together 1 cup sugar and ½ to 2 teaspoons of cinnamon. If you run out before all of the biscuits are coated, prepare more. If you end up with extra, pour the butter over the biscuits in the pan and sprinkle with the remaining cinnamon/sugar mixture. Cut biscuits in halves; roll in melted butter, then in the cinnamon sugar mixture. Drop into a greased Bundt or tube pan. Bake 30 minutes at 350 degrees. Turn out on plate.

The following is also a recipe given to me by my good friend Doreen. We first had it at a picnic we went on in the Blue Ridge Mountains of North Carolina, many years ago while visiting Doreen. It was so refreshing on a hot North Carolina day!

Lemon Crème Pie

1-6-ounce can frozen lemonade
6 ounces frozen whipped topping
1 can sweetened condensed milk
1 graham cracker crust

Combine the first 3 ingredients and pour into graham cracker crust. Refrigerate. Limeade can be substituted for lemonade. Low-fat whipped topping and fat-free sweetened condensed milk can be used instead of the regular products.

My mother made the best chocolate chip cookies ever. I'm convinced that it was her touch more than the recipe. My daughter Sarah makes this recipe now to take to outings.

Mom's Chocolate Chip Cookies

2 ¼ cups flour
1 teaspoon baking soda
1 package instant vanilla pudding
1 cup butter or butter-flavored Crisco
¼ cup sugar
¾ cup brown sugar
1 teaspoon vanilla
2 eggs
2 cups chocolate chips

Mix flour with baking soda. Combine butter, sugar, vanilla, and pudding mix in large mixing bowl. Beat until smooth and creamy. Beat in eggs. Gradually add flour mixture, then stir in about 2 cups of chocolate chips. Drop onto an ungreased baking sheet. Bake at 350 degrees for 8–10 minutes.

I remember Mom making the following cake when I was little. It was so moist and quick to make. She always frosted it with a white icing, but a peanut butter icing would be good also. To be really quick, stir a heaping spoonful of peanut butter into a can of white frosting and blend only until the peanut butter is well combined with the frosting. These days as an empty nester I buy a brand name frosting for about 87 cents a can at an Amish store.

Mayonnaise Cake

1 cup sugar
2 cups flour
4 tablespoons cocoa
2 teaspoons baking soda
a little salt

Sift together; add ¾ cup mayonnaise, 1 cup cold water, and a little vanilla. Pour into a greased and floured 8"x 8" baking pan. Bake in a 350-degree oven until toothpick inserted into center comes out clean, about 25 minutes.

The following is a recipe that my husband's Grandmother Sleeper gave me. It doesn't sound appetizing as she used to say, but it sure is good!

Ugly Bake Cake

2 cups sugar
2 teaspoons baking soda
3 cups flour
2 teaspoons salt
2 teaspoons cinnamon

Stir all together. Add:

1 ⅓ cups cooking oil
2 teaspoons vanilla
2 eggs
4 cups peeled, chopped apples
½ cup raisins
½ cup chopped nuts (optional)

Grease and flour a 9"x13" baking pan. Batter is thick. Spread in pan and bake at 325 degrees for 1½ hours. This is like a coffeecake. It's good the first day, but even better the next! It freezes well.

I used to make the following bars often when my kids were young. I made my own raspberry jam and bought peanut butter in large buckets, so I usually had the ingredients on hand.

Peanut Butter and Jam Bars

½ cup sugar
½ cup packed brown sugar
½ cup shortening
½ cup creamy peanut butter
1 egg
1 ¼ cups flour
¾ teaspoon baking soda
½ teaspoon baking powder
½ cup raspberry jam

Heat oven to 350 degrees. Mix sugars, shortening, peanut butter, and egg. Stir in flour, baking soda, and baking powder. Reserve 1 cup dough. Press remaining dough in an ungreased 9"x 13" pan; spread with jam. Crumble reserved dough and sprinkle over jam. Bake until golden brown, about 20 minutes. Cool; drizzle with glaze. Cut into bars 2"x 1½". Makes about 3 dozen bars.

Glaze:

2 tablespoons margarine or butter
1 teaspoon vanilla
1 cup confectioners' sugar
1 to 2 tablespoons hot water

Melt margarine; mix in confectioners' sugar and vanilla. Beat in hot water, 1 teaspoon at a time, until smooth and desired consistency.

The following was a recipe that my mother gave me. She made these often. I don't think she ever made rolled molasses cookies like many women used to. Dropped cookies are quicker and she was a work-at-home mom, a hairdresser with her business in our home.

Molasses Drop Cookies

½ cup cooking oil
¼ cup molasses
1 cup sugar
1 egg
¼ cup strong coffee
2 ¼ cups flour
1 teaspoon baking soda
1 teaspoon cinnamon
1 teaspoon cloves

1 teaspoon ginger
½ teaspoon salt
¾ cup raisins, nuts, or dates

Mix well. Drop by teaspoonfuls on greased cookie sheet. Bake at 350 degrees F. for 10 to 12 minutes.

Mom gave me the following recipe. It makes two 9"x 13" pans of bars. These bars are lighter in texture and not as thick as her brown sugar brownies.

Congo Bars

Beat well:
1 pound (2 ¼ cups packed) brown sugar
1 cup cooking oil
2 eggs
1 teaspoon vanilla
Sift together:
3 cups flour
½ teaspoon salt
1 teaspoon baking soda
1 cup warm coffee

Alternate the dry ingredients and coffee. Spread batter in two, greased 9" x 13" pans or large cookie sheet with sides. Top with chocolate chips and chopped nuts. Bake at 350 degrees for 25 to 30 minutes.

I love this next recipe for chocolate cake. It is quick, inexpensive (no eggs), and very moist. I probably make this cake more than any other; it can be mixed in the pan; however, I usually use a bowl. If your budget allows, keep a container of canned frosting in your pantry to use on this cake, add candy sprinkles, and it turns an ordinary cake into a more special looking dessert when you need one quick!

Crazy Cake

3 cups flour
2 cups sugar
1 teaspoon salt
1½ teaspoons baking soda
6 tablespoons cocoa
2 tablespoons vinegar
2 cups cold water
¾ cup cooking oil
2 teaspoons vanilla

Cake is mixed in the pan in which it is to be baked. Combine dry ingredients in pan. Pour liquids over the top and stir with a fork. Bake 40 to 50 minutes in a 350-degree oven. Makes a 9" x 13" cake.

Homemade Ice Cream

4 eggs
4 cups of cream
1 ¾ cups sugar
1 teaspoon vanilla
4 cups pureed fruit (sweetened)
1 cup milk

1 ½ teaspoons almond extract

This is enough for a 4-quart ice cream maker. Make sure to mix well before putting in the ice cream container.

Often Mom would make the following cake for my brother David for his birthday.

Strawberry Sparkle Cake

Use an angel food cake that was baked in a tube pan.
1 cup boiling water
1 package strawberry-flavored gelatin
1 package frozen strawberries with sugar (1 pound)
½ pint whipping cream
2 tablespoons sugar
red food coloring

Dissolve gelatin in boiling water and add frozen block of strawberries, stirring to break up and mix berries. Place cake, widest side down, on a serving plate. Cut a 1-inch layer from the top and set aside. Cut around cake one inch from outer edge to within one inch from inner edge to within one inch from the bottom. Gently remove the section of cake between the cuts, tearing it into small pieces. Fold pieces into strawberry mixture and pour it into cake shell. Place cake layer on top. Whip cream until thick. Stir in sugar and add a few drops of red food coloring until pink. Spread sweetened whipped cream over top and sides of cake. Decorate with whole strawberries, if desired. Refrigerate until served, at least 1 hour.

My special friend and Christian mentor Hilda made the following bars for a party she was having years ago. They were a hit! I believe you can use different kinds of pudding to change the flavor with great results.

Pistachio Bars

Blend together with pastry blender:
½ cup margarine, softened
1½ cups flour
Press into a greased 9"x 13" pan. Bake at 350 degrees for 15 minutes. Watch closely to prevent burning.
Place in mixing bowl:
1-8-ounce package cream cheese, softened
½ contents of 8-ounce Cool Whip
1 cup confectioners' sugar

Blend and very carefully place over first mixture.

Then take **2 small packages of instant pistachio pudding** and **3 cups milk**. Beat 3 minutes and spread over second mixture. Lastly, spread the other half of Cool Whip on top and sprinkle with chopped nuts.

Double Chocolate Crumble Bars

½ cup margarine
1 teaspoon vanilla
¾ cup sugar
¾ cup flour
¼ teaspoon baking powder
2 tablespoons cocoa
¼ teaspoon salt
2 eggs

½ cups chopped nuts (optional)

Mix all together and spread into a greased 9" x 13" pan. Bake at 350 degrees for 15 to 20 minutes, or until bars test done. Take pan from oven and spread **2 cups miniature marshmallows** over top. Bake 3 minutes more. Cool.

1 cup semisweet chocolate chips
1 cup peanut butter
1 ½ cups Rice Krispies cereal

Put chocolate chips and peanut butter in small saucepan and stir over low heat until chocolate is melted. Stir in 1 ½ cups Rice Krispies cereal. Spread over cooled bars and chill. Cut into bars. Keep refrigerated.

My good friend Gail gave the following recipe to me at my bridal shower over 36 years ago. I still have her handwritten recipe card. I know this is a very common recipe, but it's special to have it handwritten for me by Gail from so long ago.

Magic Cookie Bars

1 ½ cups graham cracker crumbs
½ cup margarine
1 can sweetened, condensed milk
1 ½ cups coconut
1 cup chocolate chips (6 ounces)
1 cup chopped nuts

Preheat oven to 350 degrees. Use greased 9"x 13" pan. Melt margarine in the pan; sprinkle the graham cracker crumbs over the butter in pan. Pour sweetened, condensed milk evenly over crumbs. Top evenly with remaining ingredients; press down gently. Bake 25 to 30 minutes, or until lightly browned. Cool thoroughly before cutting. Store, loosely covered, at room temperature.

Double Chocolate Oatmeal Cookies

1 ½ cups sugar
1 cup margarine, softened
1 egg
¼ cup water
1 teaspoon vanilla
1 ¼ cups flour
⅓ cup cocoa
½ teaspoon baking soda
½ teaspoon salt
3 cups quick-cooking oatmeal
1 package (6 ounces) chocolate chips

Heat oven to 350 degrees. Mix sugar, margarine, egg, water, and vanilla. Stir in remaining ingredients. Drop dough by rounded teaspoonfuls about 2 inches apart onto an ungreased cookie sheet. Bake until almost no indentation remains when touched, 10 to 12 minutes. Immediately remove from cookie sheet. Makes about 5 ½ dozen cookies.

Two Egg Quick Cake

2 cups flour
1 ⅓ cups sugar
2 ½ teaspoons baking powder
1 teaspoon salt
⅞ cup milk

1 ½ teaspoons vanilla
½ cup shortening
2 eggs

Sift all dry ingredients together. Mix in other ingredients. Bake in two greased layer cake pans at 350 degrees for 30 to 35 minutes. For cupcakes, bake at 375 degrees for 20 to 25 minutes.

The following is a very simple pie that can be made ahead, since it should be refrigerated before serving. I do like to keep low-fat buttermilk on hand; in most recipes that I have that call for buttermilk, it makes a significant difference rather than using plain milk. I have bought buttermilk powder, but I have not used it enough to say it is as good as the liquid that I buy.

Buttermilk Pie

1 ½ cups sugar
⅓ cup butter or margarine, melted
1 cup buttermilk
1 teaspoon vanilla
½ cup Bisquick (or homemade version)
3 eggs

Grease glass pie pan. Beat all ingredients until smooth. Pour into pan. Bake in 350 degree oven for 30 to 40 minutes, or until knife inserted in center comes out clean. Best served cold.

My friend Doreen from North Carolina gave me this next recipe. Her friend Martha had given it to her. I buy poppy seeds at the health food store; they keep best stored in the freezer.

Lemon Poppy Seed Bundt Cake

1 box white cake mix (or use lemon cake mix with vanilla pudding)
4 eggs
1 small box instant lemon pudding
¼ cup poppy seeds
¾ cup vegetable oil
1 cup water

Mix well. Grease and flour Bundt pan. Bake 40 to 45 minutes. Remove from pan immediately. Punch hole in top with meat fork. Pour topping over slowly.

Topping:

2 cups confectioners' sugar
½ cup lemon juice
2 tablespoons softened margarine

Mix well.

My sister gave me the following super moist sour cream coffee cake recipe. It is even better the day after you make it. I still use it when company is coming for coffee or Bible study.

Sour Cream Coffee Cake

½ cup brown sugar
1 tablespoon cinnamon
1 cup chopped pecans
1 yellow cake mix
¾ cup cooking oil
½ cup sugar
1 teaspoon vanilla
4 eggs
1 cup sour cream

Grease and flour Bundt pan. Combine brown sugar, cinnamon, and ½ cup pecans. Set aside. Combine cake mix, oil, sugar, vanilla, eggs, and sour cream. Beat 2 minutes on medium speed. Stir in ½ cup pecans. Pour ½ batter in pan; sprinkle with ½ brown sugar mixture. Pour in remaining batter then the rest of the brown sugar mixture. Cut through the batter so the brown sugar mixture will go through all of the cake.

Bake at 350 degrees for 45 to 50 minutes. This cake is better served cold.

My daughter Sarah used to make the following pie when she was a teenager. It is very good!

English Apple Pie

1 egg
¾ cup sugar
½ cup flour
1 teaspoon baking powder
½ teaspoon salt

1 cup chopped apple, peeled
⅓ cup chopped nuts

Beat egg and sugar together. Sift flour, baking powder, and salt and add chopped apples and nuts to the flour, then add egg mixture. Mix well. Place in glass pie plate and bake at 350 degrees for 20 to 25 minutes.

As I have said before, I rarely have unsweetened baking chocolate on hand since it is more expensive than the cocoa I buy in bulk. The next two recipes are made with cocoa; however, most of the chocolate crinkle cookie recipes I have seen call for the more expensive unsweetened baking chocolate. You can substitute cocoa for unsweetened chocolate: 1 square chocolate is the same as 3 tablespoons cocoa plus 1 tablespoon shortening.

Chocolate Crinkles

Microwave recipe

10 tablespoons butter or margarine
6 tablespoons cocoa
2 cups flour
1 cup sugar
2 teaspoons baking powder
1 teaspoon salt
2 eggs
1 teaspoon vanilla
½ cup chopped nuts, optional
confectioners' sugar

Microwave butter in medium microwave-proof bowl on

high power 45 to 60 seconds, or until melted. Add cocoa; blend well. Beat in flour, sugar, baking powder, salt, eggs, and vanilla. Stir in nuts. Refrigerate 8 hours or until firm.

Shape dough into 1-inch balls; roll in confectioners' sugar. Place 8 balls 2 inches apart in circular shape on wax paper. Microwave on medium power for 1 to 2 minutes, or until surface is dry but cookies soft. Cool. Makes about 4 dozen cookies.

Cocoa Crinkle Cookies

2 cups sugar
¾ cup cooking oil
¾ cup cocoa
4 eggs
2 teaspoons vanilla
2 ⅛ cups flour
2 teaspoons baking powder
½ teaspoon salt
confectioners' sugar

Combine sugar and oil in large bowl; add cocoa, beating until well blended. Beat in eggs and vanilla. Stir together flour, baking powder, and salt; gradually add to cocoa mixture, beating well. Cover; refrigerate until dough is firm enough to handle, at least 6 hours. Heat oven to 350 degrees. Grease cookie sheet. Shape dough into 1-inch balls; roll in powdered sugar to coat. Place about 2 inches apart on prepared cookie sheet. Bake for 10 to 13 minutes, or until almost no indentation remains when touched lightly and tops are crackled. Cool slightly. Remove from cookie sheet to wire rack. Cool completely.

Apple Danish

Pastry:

3 cups flour
½ teaspoon salt
1 cup shortening
½ cup milk
1 egg yolk

Filling:

6 cups sliced, peeled apples
1 ½ cups sugar
¼ cup butter or margarine, melted
2 tablespoons flour
1 teaspoon ground cinnamon

Glaze:

1 egg white, lightly beaten
½ cup confectioners' sugar
2 to 3 teaspoons water

In mixing bowl, combine flour and salt; cut in shortening until mixture resembles coarse crumbs. Combine egg yolk and milk; add to flour mixture. Stir just until dough clings together. Divide dough in half. On a lightly floured surface, roll half of dough into a 15"x 10"x 1" greased baking pan. Set aside. In a bowl, toss together filling ingredients; spoon over pastry in pan. Roll out remaining dough to another 15" x 10" rectangle. Place over filling. Brush with egg white. Bake at 375 degrees for 40 minutes, or until golden brown. Cool on a wire rack. Combine the confectioners' sugar and enough water to achieve a drizzling consistency. Drizzle over warm pastry. Cut into squares. Serve warm or cold. Makes 20 to 24 servings. This is one of my favorite apple recipes. This recipe is a little time intensive but worth it!

The following is one of my favorite pie recipes. It could easily be made in an 8-inch piecrust or double the ingredients and bake in a 10-inch piecrust, but adjust the cooking time.

Chocolate Chip Cookie Pie

2 eggs
½ cup flour
½ cup sugar
½ cup packed brown sugar
1 cup margarine, melted and cooled to room temperature
1 cup chocolate chips
1 cup chopped walnuts (optional)
1-9-inch unbaked piecrust
whipped cream or ice cream

Preheat oven to 325 degrees. In large bowl, beat eggs until foamy; beat in flour, sugar, and brown sugar until well blended. Blend in melted butter. Stir in chocolate chips and nuts. Pour into pie shell.

Bake at 325 degrees for approximately 1 hour. Remove from oven. Serve warm with whipped cream or ice cream.

Butter Nut Chewies

2 eggs
2 cups packed brown sugar

1 teaspoon vanilla
½ cup melted margarine or buttered-flavored
Crisco
1 ½ cups flour
2 teaspoons baking powder
½ teaspoon salt
1 cup finely chopped nuts

Preheat oven to 350 degrees. Grease 13"x 9" baking pan.

Beat eggs until light and foamy in a large bowl. Beat with electric mixer, sugar, vanilla, and margarine until creamy. Combine flour with baking powder and salt. Add to egg mixture. Mix at low speed until blended. Stir in nuts at low speed. Mixture will be stiff. Spread evenly in greased pan. Bake at 350 degrees for 25 to 30 minutes, or until top is light brown. Cool 10 to 15 minutes. Cut into bars. Makes 2 dozen.

Betty Mason, who is a great cook with years of experience, gave me this next recipe many years ago. I have used it often during apple picking season.

Apple Crisp

2 cups brown sugar
1 cup flour
1 stick margarine
cinnamon

Fill a 9"x 13" greased baking pan with peeled and cored McIntosh apple slices. Mix together brown sugar and flour, cut in margarine. Sprinkle over apple slices. Sprinkle approximately ⅛ cup of water over this. Cover with aluminum foil for a soft top or leave uncovered for a crisp top. Bake in a 350-degree oven until apples are cooked through.

My husband's Grandmother Sleeper gave this next recipe to me. This is an old-fashioned Indian pudding recipe that is made in the microwave rather than baking a long time in a conventional oven. I love the traditional New England Indian pudding but not the time it takes to bake in the oven. This way of cooking is much more economical unless you are using the old-fashioned wood cooking stove.

Microwave Indian Pudding

Place **4 cups of milk** in a 1-quart casserole dish. Heat on medium for 5 to 6 minutes, or according to your microwave instructions to scald milk. Stir in **½ cup cornmeal**. Cook on medium-high for 4 to 6 minutes, or until smooth and thickened. Stir once. In a large bowl, combine

½ cup brown sugar
½ cup molasses
2 eggs slightly beaten
2 tablespoons melted butter
1 teaspoon salt
½ teaspoon cinnamon
½ teaspoon ground ginger
dash nutmeg

Stir hot milk mixture into egg mixture. Cook in a 2-quart casserole. Bake in a microwave oven on medium for 19 to 24 minutes, or until set but still quivery on top.

I love to have cans of pumpkin on hand because it's so versatile and makes good desserts, breads, and muffins. The following is a very quick way to make pumpkin pie without taking the time to make piecrust. It also would be lower in fat than regular pumpkin pie. You can substitute fat-free evaporated milk for regular, and low-fat baking mix for regular baking mix to further lower the fat. I always try to buy canned pumpkin on sale around Thanksgiving or Christmas and stock up. If you grow pumpkins, you can cook, puree, and freeze it to last quite a long time.

Crazy Pumpkin Pie

2 eggs
¾ cup sugar
1-12-ounce can evaporated milk plus water to make
2 cups liquid
¼ teaspoon cloves
½ teaspoon ginger
1 teaspoon cinnamon
¼ teaspoon nutmeg
½ teaspoon salt
1 ½ cups cooked, mashed, or canned pumpkin
½ cup dry biscuit mix

Place all ingredients in blender and blend on medium speed about 3 minutes. Pour into greased 10-inch glass pie pan. Bake in a 350-degree oven 45 to 50 minutes, or until knife inserted in middle comes out clean. Serve cold with sweetened whipped cream or vanilla ice cream.

The following is a recipe that my mother gave me. It takes less time to cook than the usual apple pie making it an excellent time saver. This is the only way my daughter Sarah makes apple pie. We use McIntosh apples for best results.

Mom's Apple Pie

One double unbaked piecrust. Make sure to use a glass 9-inch pie plate. Fill with peeled, cored, and sliced apples combined with 1 ¼ cups sugar. Sprinkle with apple pie seasoning, about 1 teaspoon. Cover with vented top piecrust. Bake for 10 minutes on high in microwave oven, and then transfer to a conventional oven for 10 minutes at 450 degrees.

Dump Cake

- **1 large can crushed pineapple with juice**
- **1 can pie filling (we like cherry)**
- **1 box cake mix (white or yellow)**
- **1 ½ sticks margarine**

Butter a 9"x 13" pan. Turn pineapple and pie filling into pan. Spread *dry* cake mix all over fruit. Slice 1½ sticks margarine over dry cake mix. Bake 1 hour at 350 degrees. Serve lukewarm or cold. Top with vanilla ice cream. Makes 12 servings.

The following bread pudding has always been a favorite dessert at our house. It's inexpensive to make, quick to put together, and yummy like French toast with syrup. It's a good way to use up bread ends or stale bread.

Double Boiler Bread Pudding

Into a double boiler put these ingredients in the order given (do not stir): **1 cup brown sugar; 4 slices bread, buttered and cubed; 3 eggs beaten and added to 3 cups of milk flavored with 1 teaspoon vanilla.** Cook over boiling water 1 hour. Turn upside down on a serving plate, serve warm plain, or with whipped cream.

The following recipe is one my sister Bev used a lot and so have I over the years. It can be doubled. I like how quick and easy this recipe is!

Peanut Butter No Bake Cookies

1 stick margarine
2 cups sugar
½ cup evaporated milk or regular milk
1 teaspoon vanilla

Place above in top of double boiler, cook for 15 minutes. Add:

1 cup peanut butter
3 cups quick-cooking oatmeal

Drop by tablespoonful onto wax paper or pour into 7" x 11" buttered pan.

My daughter Sarah loves the following recipe. It is a very moist cookie and makes a large amount. I have made these cookies for many years.

Pumpkin Cookies

1 can pumpkin (canned squash works also)
2 eggs
1 cup oil (scant)
2 teaspoons cinnamon
1 teaspoon salt
2 teaspoons vanilla
2 cups sugar
4 teaspoons baking powder
4 cups flour
2 teaspoons baking soda in 2 teaspoons milk
12 ounces chocolate chips

Mix together and drop by teaspoonfuls onto cookie sheets. Bake at 350 degrees for about 10 minutes. 2 cups cooked, mashed pumpkin can be used instead of a can of pumpkin.

Peanut Butter Cookies

1 egg
½ cup sugar
½ cup brown sugar
½ cup vegetable oil
½ cup peanut butter
1 teaspoon vanilla
1 teaspoon baking soda
½ teaspoon salt
1½ cups flour

Beat all together. Shape into balls size of a walnut. Place on a cookie sheet and press out flat with a fork. Bake at 350 degrees for about 10 minutes. Don't overbake!

I usually doubled this recipe.

I'm sure my mother must have made the following bars hundreds of times over the years. My nephew Kevin especially liked Mom to make a batch for him.

Scotch-A-Roos

Bring just to a boil:
1 cup sugar
1 cup white Karo syrup
Do not let boil. Remove from heat and add:
1 cup peanut butter

Stir until melted.
Add:

6 cups Rice Krispies

Spread in 9" x 13" greased pan.
Melt 6-ounce package chocolate chips with 6-ounce package butterscotch chips.
Frost bars, cool, and cut into squares.

Microwave Apple Crunch Pie

1-9-inch microwave cooked or baked pie shell with fluted edge

Filling:

5 to 6 cups peeled, sliced apples
1 tablespoon lemon juice
½ cup sugar

2 tablespoons flour
½ teaspoon cinnamon
Toss together and pile high in pie shell.
Topping:
   ¼ cup margarine or butter
   ½ cup flour
   ¼ cup brown or white granulated sugar
   ½ teaspoon cinnamon

Cut butter into other topping ingredients until crumbly. Sprinkle evenly over filling. Place wax paper under plate while microwaving. Microwave on high 8 to 14 minutes until apples are tender.

There is nothing better than that first rhubarb dessert in the spring as rhubarb becomes available. Most country homes in my hometown in Maine have a patch of rhubarb growing somewhere on the grounds. It's easy to pick, clean, and freeze for use later in the year and for rhubarb jam!

Easy Rhubarb Dessert

   4 cups sliced fresh or frozen rhubarb
   1-3-ounce package raspberry gelatin
   ⅓ cup sugar
   1-18¼-ounce yellow or white cake mix
   1 cup water
   ⅓ cup margarine, melted

Place the cut-up rhubarb in a greased 9" x 13" baking pan. Sprinkle with the combined gelatin, sugar, and *dry* cake mix. Pour water evenly over dry ingredients; drizzle with margarine. Bake at 350 degrees for 1 hour, or until rhubarb is tender. Top with ice cream if desired.

My next recipe is not one I used to make for my children, but one I came across a few years ago for chocolate chip cookies that I really like. I got the recipe from a package of Crisco butter-flavored all-vegetable shortening sticks.

Ultimate Chocolate Chip Cookies

¾ cup butter-flavored Crisco
1 ¼ cups firmly packed light brown sugar
2 tablespoons milk
1 tablespoon vanilla
1 egg
1¾ cups all-purpose flour
1 teaspoon salt
¾ teaspoon baking soda
1 cup semisweet chocolate chips
1 cup coarsely chopped pecans (optional)*

Heat oven to 375 degrees. Place sheets of foil on countertop for cooling cookies. I bake my cookies on parchment paper, and then slide the paper with the cookies onto cooling racks instead of using foil. The cookie sheets don't have to be washed when using parchment paper.

Combine butter-flavored Crisco, brown sugar, milk, and vanilla in large bowl. Beat at medium speed until well blended. Beat egg into creamed mixture. Combine flour, salt, and baking soda. Mix into creamed mixture just until blended. Stir in chocolate chips and pecan pieces.

Drop rounded tablespoon of dough 3 inches apart onto ungreased baking sheet. Bake one baking sheet at a time at

375 degrees for 8 to 10 minutes for chewy cookies, or 11 to 13 minutes for crisp cookies. *Do not overbake.* Cool 2 minutes on baking sheet. Remove cookies to foil to cool completely. Makes about 3 dozen cookies. I always double this recipe, freeze some, or give away a batch.

*If nuts are omitted, add an additional ½ cup semisweet chocolate chips.

The following is such a simple recipe and you can use any berry or mixed berries. It looks nice served in a parfait glass with ice cream or whipped cream on top. It makes a simple dessert look and taste like an elegant dessert! Cake mixes are one of the few prepared mixes that I like in my pantry because of their versatility in baking. I can often find it for around 75 cents a box for the double-layer size.

Blueberry Dump Cake

1 box yellow cake mix
4 cups fresh or frozen blueberries
½ cup white sugar
½ cup butter or margarine, melted
1 teaspoon cinnamon

Preheat oven to 350 degrees. Mix berries, sugar, and cinnamon in the bottom of a 9"x 13" pan. Cover berries with dry cake mix. Pour butter over cake mix; do not stir. Bake for 30 minutes, or until light brown and bubbly around the edges. Serve warm or cold. Top with ice cream.

The following is a good Fourth of July dessert idea because it is red, white, and blue. It's also very low in fat.

Very Berry Cheesecake Trifle

2-8-ounce packages fat-free cream cheese, softened
¾ cup powdered sugar
1 teaspoon vanilla or almond extract
1-8-ounce container fat-free whipped topping
1 prepared angel food cake
1-21- ounce can strawberry pie filling
1-21-ounce can blueberry pie filling

In a large bowl with mixer on low, beat softened cream cheese, powdered sugar, and extract for 2 minutes until well blended. Add cool whip and continue mixing for another minute, or until well blended. With a spatula, stir in bite-sized pieces of angel food cake. Using a large glass bowl or trifle bowl, spread strawberry pie filling evenly over the bottom of the bowl. Next, spread cream cheese cake mixture evenly over strawberry layer. Spread the blueberry pie filling evenly over cream cheese/cake mixture. Ready to serve or refrigerate until ready to eat. Makes 15 servings.

I think I have been making the following recipe since I was a teenager. I find that in Pennsylvania they are sometimes called something different. Either way, they are yummy!

Whoopie Pies

Cream together:
½ cup shortening

1 cup sugar

Add:

2 egg yolks, beaten until light-colored

Sift together:

5 tablespoons cocoa
2 cups sifted flour
1 teaspoon baking powder
1 teaspoon baking soda
1 teaspoon salt

Add alternately to creamed mixture with:

1 cup milk
1 teaspoon vanilla

Drop by teaspoonfuls onto ungreased cookie sheets. Bake at 350 degrees for 8 to 10 minutes, depending upon the size cookie you make. Cool cookies, then put together with the following filling.

Whoopie Pie Filling

½ cup shortening
2 cups confectioners' sugar
2 egg whites, beaten until stiff
¼ teaspoon salt
1 teaspoon vanilla

I usually substitute marshmallow fluff for the egg whites. You can use egg white powder. Cream shortening. Add the confectioners' sugar, salt, vanilla, and marshmallow fluff. Beat with electric beaters until smooth.

Dump Bars

Into the top of a double boiler put:
 2 sticks margarine
 1 teaspoon vanilla
 1 pound light brown sugar
 ½ teaspoon salt
 4 beaten eggs

After dumping these ingredients into top of double boiler, place over boiling water. Stir occasionally so that the eggs are mixed into ingredients thoroughly. Only heat and stir until the margarine is melted. Remove top of double boiler from the stove and dump in:

 2 cups sifted flour
 1 teaspoon baking powder

Beat well and turn into a greased 9"x 13" pan. Sprinkle the top with about **1 cup of chocolate chips**. Bake at 325 degrees for 40 minutes. Cool in pan then cut and remove. They freeze and keep well! They are also good with the addition of chopped walnuts. These bars are another version of butterscotch brownies or blonde brownies.

The following apple dumplings will melt in your mouth. Anyone who likes apple pie will love these with vanilla ice cream. This recipe makes a large amount and can be made a day ahead and refrigerated then heated just before serving. The pastry is so tender!

Apple Dumplings

3 cups sugar
¼ teaspoon nutmeg
3 cups water
6 tablespoons butter
1 teaspoon cinnamon

Make into a syrup, boiling about 3 minutes. Cover while making dumplings.

Using **6 to 8 good-sized apples,** (I use McIntosh) peel, core and slice into fairly thin slices. Set aside.

4 cups flour
2 teaspoons salt
4 teaspoons baking powder
1½ cups shortening
1 cup milk

Using a pastry blender, cut shortening into dry ingredients until it has the appearance of pea-sized clumps. Mix in milk to form dough that you can roll out into ¼-inch thickness. Cut into 5-inch squares. Place several apple slices onto the middle of each square of dough. Bring corners of dough pieces to center, making a secure ball. Place dumplings in a baking dish (I usually use a glass one) that has been lightly sprayed with nonstick spray. Pour syrup over the top and bake at 375 degrees for 35 to 40 minutes. Top with vanilla ice cream and enjoy.

My mother used to make the following ice cream when I was still at home. It tastes like fudgsicles!

Homemade Chocolate Ice Cream

5 cups milk
5 squares unsweetened chocolate
5 tablespoons flour
2½ to 3 cups sugar
¾ teaspoon salt
3 eggs
2 large cans evaporated milk
2 teaspoons vanilla

Scald milk. Melt chocolate. Mix melted chocolate with sugar, flour, and salt then mix beaten eggs in. Mix that mixture into scalded milk, adding canned evaporated milk and vanilla last. Refrigerate until cool, then freeze as directed in ice cream maker. This makes 4 quarts ice cream. For a 3-quart ice cream maker, reduce by ½.

Ooey-Gooey Peanut Butter Chocolate Brownies

¾ cup fat-free sweetened, condensed milk, divided
¼ cup butter or margarine, melted and cooled
¼ cup fat-free milk
1 box devil's food cake mix
1 large egg white, lightly beaten
cooking spray
1-7-ounce jar marshmallow fluff or about 1¾ cups
½ cup peanut butter chips

Preheat oven to 350 degrees.

Combine ¼ cup sweetened, condensed milk, butter, and

next 3 ingredients in a bowl (batter will be stiff). Spray bottom of a 9" x 13" baking pan with cooking spray. Press ⅔ of batter into prepared pan using floured hands; pat evenly (layer will be thin).

Bake at 350 degrees for 10 minutes. Combine ½ cup sweetened, condensed milk and marshmallow fluff in a bowl; stir in chips. Spread marshmallow mixture evenly over brownie layer. Carefully drop remaining brownie batter by spoonfuls over marshmallow mixture. Bake at 350 degrees for 30 minutes. Cool completely in pan on a wire rack. Makes 2 dozen brownies.

The following is a little different from my recipe for chocolate chip cookie pie. I actually like this one better. It's the recipe from the back of Nestle chocolate chips.

Toll House Cookie Pie

1 unbaked 9-inch pie shell
2 large eggs
½ cup all-purpose flour
½ cup granulated sugar
½ cup packed brown sugar
1 ½ sticks butter, softened
1 cup chocolate chips
1 cup chopped nuts

Beat eggs on high until foamy. Beat in flour, granulated sugar, and brown sugar. Beat in butter. Stir in chocolate chips and nuts. Spoon into unbaked pie shell.

Bake in a preheated 325-degree oven for 55 to 60 minutes, or until a knife comes out clean when inserted halfway between outside edge and the center. Serve warm with ice cream.

Candy, Jelly, Jam, and Preserves

Lemon curd is a recipe that is very easy to make; however to buy it, often you need to go to the gourmet section of your supermarket. At an English tea you would find this served with scones; I like it with biscuits and for the filling in Linzer cookies. I have made both of these lemon curd recipes, but I like the second one better.

Lemon Curd #1

- ½ cup sugar
- 1 tablespoon cornstarch
- 2 teaspoons finely shredded lemon peel
- ½ cup lemon juice
- 2 tablespoons margarine or butter
- 3 beaten egg yolks

In a saucepan, stir together sugar and cornstarch. Stir in peel, juice, and margarine. Cook and stir until thickened and bubbly. Gradually stir about half of the hot mixture into yolks. Return all to saucepan. Bring to a gentle boil. Cook and stir for 2 minutes more. Cover surface with clear plastic wrap. Cool; chill before using. Makes 1 cup. Lemon curd can be stored in the refrigerator for up to 1 week. This recipe can be doubled and freeze half of it in the freezer. Thaw in the refrigerator and use within 1 week.

The following lemon curd recipe makes more and is so easy to make. I usually make this one now instead of the previous one. It's great to fill Linzer cookies.

Lemon Curd #2

4 eggs
2 cups sugar
⅛ teaspoon salt
½ cup lemon juice (3 large lemons)
2 tablespoons grated lemon zest
¼ cup butter

Beat together first 3 ingredients. Stir in butter, lemon juice, and lemon zest. Cook in the top of a double boiler until thick, about 20 to 25 minutes, stirring frequently. Cool to room temperature, then store in the refrigerator. This makes about 1½ cups.

Fantasy Fudge

3 cups sugar
¾ cups butter, no substitutes
5 ounces evaporated milk
1 teaspoon vanilla
1-12-ounce bag chocolate chips
1-7-ounce jar marshmallow fluff

Combine sugar, butter, and milk. Bring to a boil slowly and when it starts to boil, time for 5 minutes. Remove from heat and stir in chocolate chips, stirring until melted. Add marshmallow fluff and vanilla. Mix well. Pour into a buttered 9"x 13" pan.

The following is my favorite fudge recipe. The recipe makes a 5-pound batch. It is soft but not too soft. Probably this is my most requested recipe; it is practically a no-fail fudge!

Peanut Butter Fudge

1 pound package brown sugar
1 pound package confectioners' sugar
1 stick margarine or butter
1 cup canned, evaporated milk
2 cups (12 ounces) peanut butter
1-7-ounce jar marshmallow fluff

Combine sugars, margarine, and milk in large pan. Bring to a boil slowly and continue boiling for 7 minutes. Stir frequently. Remove from heat and stir in peanut butter and marshmallow until dissolved. I use a wire whisk to do this. Pour in 9"x 13" buttered pan. Makes 5 pounds fudge. My friend Doreen likes me to put M & M's in it. This has to be done just before you pour it into the buttered pan or they will melt.

Pecan Turtles

½ pound pecan halves
1-14-ounce bag caramels, unwrapped
1-9-ounce package milk chocolate kisses, unwrapped

On a lightly greased cookie sheet, arrange 5 pecan halves to resemble turtle's 4 feet and a head. Place one caramel in center of each turtle. Continue until there are no more spare parts. Place cookie sheet in preheated 325-degree oven until caramels have softened, about 5 minutes.

Remove from oven. With a buttered spatula, flatten caramels over pecans. Place a chocolate kiss on each turtle. Chocolate will soften from the heat of the caramels. Transfer turtles to waxed paper to cool.

The following raspberry jam recipe is one that I have made for many years. It does not use pectin and has great flavor.

Raspberry Jam

4 cups raspberries
4 cups sugar

Hull and wash raspberries, drain well. Place in a large saucepan. Mash slightly to extract juice.

Cook gently in its own juice for 5 minutes. Add the sugar and bring slowly to a boil, stirring until sugar is dissolved. Boil rapidly for 20 minutes, being careful not to burn. If using a candy thermometer, cook until reaching 220 degrees. Pour into hot sterilized jars and seal with melted paraffin wax. Makes four 8-ounce jars.

Microwave Apple Jelly

1-6-ounce can frozen apple juice concentrate, defrosted
1 package powdered fruit pectin
2 cups hot tap water

3¾ cups sugar

In a 3-quart casserole dish, blend together apple juice and pectin. Stir in water. Cover. Microwave at high 8 to 9 minutes, stirring well after 4 minutes, until bubbles form around edge of dish.

Add sugar, mixing well. Cover. Microwave at high 6 to 8 minutes, stirring well after 4 minutes, until mixture boils. Time for 1 minute of boiling. Stir and skim off foam with spoon. Ladle into sterilized canning jars and seal. Makes about 4 cups. Grape juice concentrate can be used instead of apple.

Penuche or Brown Sugar Fudge

1 pound light brown sugar
½ teaspoon salt
1 cup white sugar
4 tablespoons flour
1 cup evaporated milk
Lump of butter
2 heaping tablespoons marshmallow fluff
1 teaspoon vanilla
½ cup chopped walnuts

Mix first five ingredients in saucepan. When they reach a full rolling boil, boil exactly 5 minutes, stirring constantly. Remove from heat. Add lump of butter, marshmallow fluff, vanilla, and nuts. Beat until creamy. Turn into buttered 9"x 13" pan. Spread. Cool. Cut and enjoy!

A needham is a coconut, potato candy with a chocolate coating that we used to be able to buy at the local store. In Maine many people make the homemade version. My mother made homemade needhams to give away every Christmas season. She made many batches because they are a popular treat. Now that my mom is no longer living, I'm sure many friends think of her lovingly at Christmas time, missing her and her homemade needhams.

Homemade Needhams

¾ **cup mashed potato**
½ **teaspoon salt**
2-1-pound packages confectioners' sugar
1 stick margarine
½ **pound sweetened flaked coconut**
2 teaspoons vanilla

Peel and cook potato to make ¾ cup mashed potato (not seasoned). Add salt. Using a double boiler, place stick of margarine in it and melt over boiling water. Add mashed potato, confectioners' sugar, flaked coconut, and vanilla.

Mix well, then turn into a buttered jellyroll pan. Spread evenly. Put in a cool place to harden. When firm, cut into small squares and dip in the following chocolate mixture.

Chocolate Dip Coating

1-12-ounce package chocolate chips
4 squares unsweetened chocolate
½ **cake paraffin (2 ½"x 2 ½")**

Use double boiler. Place paraffin in top over boiling water to melt. Then add the two kinds of chocolate. Allow chocolate to melt. Stir well to mix ingredients. Using a toothpick or candy dipping fork, dip individual needham. Hold each square above chocolate mixture after dipping so the square drains well. Place on waxed paper to harden. This makes about 66 good-sized needhams.

Peanut Butter Balls

1 cup confectioners' sugar
1 cup graham cracker crumbs
1 cup peanut butter
pinch of salt

Knead these ingredients together with your hands. Make into small balls.

Melt together in top of double boiler over water that is simmering:

1-6-ounce package chocolate chips
1-1½"x 2" piece of paraffin

Use a toothpick or candy-dipping tool to dip each peanut butter ball into chocolate mixture. Let the excess chocolate drip off then place peanut butter ball on wax paper for hardening.

My good friend Rhoda Brenneman, who also happens to be Amish, is a great cook. Every year during tomato season she goes to the local nursing home to cook some of her homemade ketchup for the residents to taste and reminisce about days gone by when they preserved their own bountiful gardens. French fries are cooked for the residents to have with the ketchup. This is a very popular annual activity that the residents, staff, and Rhoda look forward to each year. I absolutely love her ketchup so I asked her if I could have the recipe for my book. She did give me the recipe, but I'm sure it won't taste exactly the same because she doesn't measure her ingredients exact. After taste testing, I'm sure she tweaks the recipe for better flavor.

Rhoda's Ketchup

Cut up: **1 bushel tomatoes**
  8 onions

Cook until soft, then run through a juicer. Pour into a jelly bag and drip all night.

Take pulp and put in a heavy saucepan and add:

10 cups sugar
½ cup salt
2 quarts vinegar
1 tablespoon celery seed

Bring to a boil. Make a little bag and put scant **1 cup mixed pickling spice** and tie shut and pitch into the tomatoes. Simmer together for 40 minutes. Take two spoons and squeeze all juice out of the spice bag that is possible. Discard bag.

Put ketchup in canning jars and process for 20 minutes.

Beverages and Miscellaneous

The following is such a good smoothie recipe, but I never make it the same. Sometimes I change the berries, yogurt flavor or amounts. Sometimes I add ice cream. Usually we add sugar or artificial sweetener, not honey.

Berry Smoothies

1 cup blueberries
10 or more whole frozen strawberries
1 cup strawberry yogurt
1 cup milk
2 tablespoons sugar, honey, or artificial sweetener equivalent

Blend together well in blender. Makes enough for 2 large servings.

Cinnamon Christmas Decorations

Mix:

24 tablespoons cinnamon
1 cup applesauce

Use cinnamon when rolling out mixture. Roll out quite thick, cut shapes such as hearts or gingerbread men and women with cookie cutters. Use a straw to make a hole for hanging. Let air dry for a day or two. Use narrow ribbon for hanging.

Sun Tea

Put 9 regular-sized tea bags in a clean gallon glass jar and fill with cold water. Cap loosely and place in hot sunshine, away from combustible material, for three to four hours. You can vary the number of tea bags and the duration of brewing according to the tea strength you desire. Remove the tea bags. Sweeten to taste with sugar or artificial sweetener. Serve over ice. Refrigerate within 5 hours of brewing start.

Hot Mulled Cider

2 quarts apple cider
½ cup brown sugar
¼ teaspoon salt
1 teaspoon whole cloves
3-inch stick cinnamon
1 teaspoon whole allspice

Combine cider, brown sugar, and salt in saucepan. Tie spices in a small piece of cheesecloth or disposable coffee filter. Cover; simmer slowly for 20 minutes. Remove spices. Serve hot. If desired, float clove-studded orange slices in cider.

The following recipe is a very tasty substitute for store-bought popsicles.

Frozen Popsicles

1 package Jell-O (any fruit flavor)
1 envelope Kool Aid (same as Jell-O flavor)
1 cup sugar
2 cups boiling water
2 cups cold water

Dissolve Jell-O, Kool Aid, and sugar in boiling water. Add cold water. Pour into popsicle makers (or small plastic cups with sticks) and freeze until firm.

Sugar Molds

2 cups sugar
4 teaspoons water

Knead ingredients for 1 minute. Pack into molds and scrape smooth. Unmold carefully, placing on a cookie sheet lined with parchment paper. Bake in 200-degree oven for 5 minutes. Sugar can be colored before mixing with water. I made these in number and letter molds to decorate birthday cakes. Once the sugar is dried they keep for a long time if kept in a dry place in an airtight container. This is an easy project to make with kids!

Pumpkin Seeds

This is a recipe for the seeds you take out of pumpkins when making jack-o'-lanterns in the fall. Steam seeds. Stir-fry in small amount of cooking oil until crisp, 5 to 10 minutes, drain on paper towels. Salt. Enjoy.

I have also done them in the oven on a cookie sheet at 350

degrees for 15 minutes, stirring every 5 minutes. Make sure after you remove the seeds from the pumpkin you clean off (don't wash) the stringy substance before steaming.

 The following recipe for crazy crunch popcorn is one that my sister would make when she was in high school. I have made it into popcorn balls or just broken it into pieces when it has nearly hardened.

Crazy Crunch Popcorn

2 quarts plain popped corn
2 cups pecans or mixed nuts
1 ⅛ cups sugar
1 cup margarine or butter
½ cup light corn syrup
1 teaspoon vanilla

Mix popped corn and nuts on a large greased cookie sheet. Combine sugar, margarine, and corn syrup in a 1½-quart saucepan. Bring to a boil over medium heat, stirring constantly. Continue boiling, stirring occasionally 10 to 15 minutes, or until mixture turns a light caramel color. Remove from heat. Stir in vanilla. Pour over popped corn and nuts. Mix to coat well. Spread out to harden. Break apart and store in tightly covered containers. Makes about 2 pounds. I have used 2 regular-sized bags of microwave light popcorn with good results.

My recipe for gorp or trail mix has been an old favorite of ours for taking on mountain hikes. It's probably best to not include prunes in the dry fruit mix, as one friend informed me after I had shared it with her on a daylong hike!

Gorp

1 cup quick-cooking rolled oats
1 cup dry roasted peanuts
½ cup shredded coconut
¼ cup wheat germ
½ cup honey
2 tablespoons cooking oil
1 cup M & M's
½ cup coarsely chopped mixed dried fruit
½ cup raisins

In a bowl combine oats, peanuts, coconut, and wheat germ. Combine honey and oil; stir into oat mixture. Spread out in a 9"x 9" pan. Bake in 300-degree oven for 30 to 40 minutes, or till light brown, stirring every 15 minutes. Remove from oven. Transfer to another greased pan; cool without stirring. Break up large pieces; stir in candy pieces, dried fruit, and raisins. Store in a tightly covered container or plastic bag. Makes 6 cups. I used to double this recipe to share with friends while hiking.

Cooking Bacon in the Oven

Preheat oven to 400 degrees. I line a large, heavy baking sheet (raised sides) with parchment paper and layer strips of bacon in single layers on the baking sheet. For 1 pound of bacon it takes 2 large baking sheets with sides. I bake thick-slab bacon for about 20 minutes and regular-sliced about 18 minutes. Rotate the pans once during cooking. Remove from oven, take the bacon off the parchment paper, and drain on a platter covered with paper towels. Once the pans have cooled you can remove the parchment paper with much of the grease and bacon particles. It's very easy to clean the pans. Sometimes I place the bacon on cooling racks on the parchment-covered baking pans to cook.

Mixes

Homemade Biscuit Mix

8 cups flour
1 ⅓ cups powdered milk
5 tablespoons baking powder
1 tablespoon salt
1 cup shortening

Blend ingredients together with a pastry blender and store in a tightly covered container in a dry area. This makes 11 cups of mix. You can substitute this mix in any Bisquick recipe. To make pancakes, use:

2 cups homemade biscuit mix
2 eggs
1 cup water or milk

Fat-Free Biscuit Mix

9 cups flour
1 cup plus 2 tablespoons dry powdered milk
¾ cup baking powder

4 teaspoons salt

Use in recipes calling for biscuit mix.
Makes 11 cups.

The following is a good way to prepare garlic bread, especially if you have unexpected company for dinner and need to come up with something quick. I have even taken hot dog buns or just sliced bread from the freezer, quickly thawed, and used the spread to make quick garlic bread. This might be a good recipe to tape to the inside of your cupboard if you use it regularly; we do.

Garlic Bread Spread

1 stick margarine or butter
2 teaspoons garlic powder
1 teaspoon onion salt
1 teaspoon dried parsley flakes

Blend together and spread on slices of French bread; split hot dog buns, toast, etc. Broil under broiler until bubbly. Shredded cheese or grated Parmesan cheese can be added before broiling also for a tasty addition. I have substituted finely minced garlic from a jar for the garlic powder with good results.

Homemade Pumpkin Pie Spice

4 teaspoons ground cinnamon
2 teaspoons ground ginger
1 teaspoon ground cloves
½ teaspoon ground nutmeg

Combine all ingredients. Store in an airtight container.

When the kids were still at home we used to go through a lot of hot cocoa mix. I started trying different homemade mix recipes to see if I could make hot cocoa mix cheaper with what I had on hand. This is one recipe that I came up with that we liked.

Hot Cocoa Mix

2 ½ cups instant nonfat dry milk
1 cup baking cocoa
1 cup sugar
½ cup nondairy powdered creamer
¼ teaspoon salt
2 cups confectioners' sugar
1 cup miniature marshmallows (optional)

In a large bowl, mix well all ingredients. Store airtight in cool, dry place. Use within 6 months. Makes about 7 cups of mix. I would usually double this recipe!

To make one serving, stir 3 generous tablespoons into 8 ounces of hot water or milk.

Sweetened Condensed Milk # 1

1 cup water
¼ cup butter or margarine
2 cups sugar
4 cups instant nonfat milk powder

Combine water and sugar in medium saucepan. Stir over

medium heat until sugar dissolves. Pour mixture in blender. Add butter or margarine. Blend on low, gradually adding milk powder. Blend on medium until smooth. Makes about 3 ½ cups or the equivalent of two 14-ounce cans of sweetened condensed milk. Omit the butter for fat-free sweetened, condensed milk. Store in the refrigerator for 1 week, or freeze the extra for up to 6 months.

Sweetened Condensed Milk # 2

1 cup instant nonfat dry milk
⅓ cup boiling water
⅔ cup granulated sugar
3 tablespoons butter or margarine

Combine all ingredients in blender; process until smooth. Store in refrigerator until ready to use. Makes about 1¼ cups.

Taco or Chili Seasoning Mix

2 tablespoons chili powder
1 tablespoon seasoned salt
2 teaspoons cumin
1 teaspoon oregano
1 teaspoon salt
1 teaspoon onion powder
½ teaspoon garlic powder

Mix and store in airtight container. This makes about ¼ cup. Use approximately 2 tablespoons per recipe. I use this for taco meat, enchiladas, and chili in place of 1 package of chili, taco, or enchilada seasoning.

My friend Jenelle shared this recipe for homemade baby wipes with me so I could share the recipe with my daughter Sarah who had 4-month-old Connor at that time. As any mother knows, this can be a real money saver. Jenelle says that she tweaked the original recipe until she had it the way she wanted it.

Jenelle's Baby Wipes

1 roll Bounty paper towels (Sarah says a large roll works best)

Cut the roll in half so you have 2 short rolls. Take the cardboard roll out of the middle of the roll. Mix together:
2½ cups warm water
2½ tablespoons baby bath or baby shampoo
1 tablespoon baby oil.

Put one of the cut paper towel rolls into a large empty wipes container (or any container that you might have that seals) and pour liquid over the roll, turning to coat all of roll. Sarah says that when using an old wipes container, the wipes pull up just as easy as purchased wipes do. Jenelle said that if a baby doesn't have a sensitivity to the baby bath, shampoo, or baby oil; then the baby shouldn't have a sensitivity to these homemade wipes.

Italian Salad Dressing Mix

1 teaspoon Italian seasoning
1 teaspoon sugar
½ teaspoon garlic powder
½ teaspoon salt
½ teaspoon onion powder

To make salad dressing, add mix with ¼ cup vinegar, 3 table-spoons water in a jar with a tight-fitting lid. Shake well until thoroughly blended. Add: **½ cup oil** and shake again until well blended. For low-fat dressing, use **¼ cup water** and **¼ cup oil** instead of **½ cup oil.**

Mixes are nice to give as a housewarming or welcome-to-the-neighborhood gift. I have given this next one. Place the mix in a sturdy plastic bag. I have sewed simple muslin bags and stenciled with an appropriate design on the bag. Hand write or type the recipe and attach it to the bag with ribbon or raffia, closing the top of the bag.

Brownie Mix

6 cups flour
8 cups sugar
4 teaspoons baking powder
2 ⅔ cups cocoa
4 teaspoons salt
2 cups vegetable shortening

In a large bowl, combine first 5 ingredients. With pastry blender, cut in shortening until evenly distributed. Store in a

large airtight container in cupboard. Keeps 10 to 12 weeks.
Makes about 17 cups of mix.

To make the brownies:

2½ cups brownie mix
2 eggs, beaten
1 teaspoon vanilla
½ cup chopped nuts (optional)

In a mixing bowl, combine first 4 ingredients. Beat with
spoon until smooth. Spread into a greased 8-inch square
baking pan. Bake at 350 degrees for 20 to 25 minutes, or
until top tests done. Makes 9 brownies.

As I have mentioned earlier in this book, one way I used
to cut items from my grocery list is to make some products
myself. The following recipe is one that I have used here and
while living in Honduras. I buy onion flakes in a 28-ounce
container, which lasts a long time. This recipe has only two
ingredients. What could be easier?

Homemade Onion Soup Mix

Equivalent to 1 packet onion soup mix:

4 beef bouillon cubes or 4 teaspoons beef bouillon
powder
3 tablespoons onion flakes

We love the following croutons and they are quick and simple to make.

Homemade Croutons

6 cups bread cubes
½ cup melted butter or olive oil
2 teaspoons Italian seasoning, ½ teaspoon garlic salt, onion salt, or whatever flavor you desire
2 teaspoons grated Parmesan cheese

If using butter, melt in microwave. Toss butter or olive oil, bread cubes, and seasonings, except grated Parmesan cheese, in a medium glass microwave-safe bowl. Microwave about 1 minute at a time, stirring between microwaving. Microwave until almost crispy. Separate cubes as you stir each time. When done, spread on wax paper to cool, sprinkle immediately with the grated Parmesan cheese. Store in a freezer container and freeze what you won't be using right away. By using the microwave, you are using less energy than by making croutons in the oven or on the stovetop.

Homemade Breadcrumbs

Save day-old, the ends, and pieces of bread, homemade or purchased. Keep in a plastic bag in the freezer. When you have a good supply, place in a single layer on a cookie sheet, thaw and place in the oven on a low temperature (250 degrees) until dry and crispy, about 20 minutes. Cool. Place in plastic bag and crush with a rolling pin or place in a blender on high until it becomes crumbs. Store your breadcrumbs in a plastic freezer bag or plastic container in the freezer. Remove crumbs as needed. These are quick and inexpensive to make. Make them while you are working in the kitchen getting a meal.

For Italian breadcrumbs:

2 cups breadcrumbs
¼ cup Parmesan cheese
2 teaspoons dried parsley flakes
1 teaspoon oregano
1 teaspoon basil
1 teaspoon garlic powder

Combine all ingredients and store in an airtight container. I store these in the freezer and take out as needed.

Seasoned Salt

1 cup salt
1 ½ teaspoons oregano
2 ½ teaspoons paprika
1 teaspoon garlic powder
2 teaspoons dry mustard
½ teaspoon onion powder

Mix and store in airtight container.

Ketchup Substitute

1-8-ounce can tomato sauce
½ cup brown sugar
2 tablespoons vinegar

Blend together until brown sugar has dissolved. This recipe would be okay in a pinch, but is a thin substitution.

Recipe Index

Appetizers, Pickles, and Relish

Soups, Salads, Dressings, and Sauces

Main Dishes

Vegetables

Breads, Rolls, and Muffins

Desserts

Candy, Jelly, Jam, and Preserves

Beverages and Miscellaneous

Mixes

Recipe Index

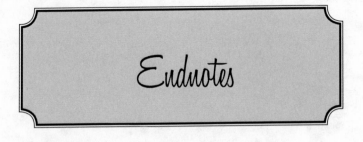

Endnotes

1. Webster's New World Dictionary, Concise Edition, 1962 by The World Publishing Company

2. Mary Jane's Cookbook from the Heart of America by Mary Jane Remole. Published in 1993 by SMITHMARK Publishers Inc.